Suddenly

my journey from terror to the
miraculous

ADA MADISON

I dedicate this book to
JT and Dad.
I thank God for second chances,
and for gifting me with the
best Son and Dad in the world.

I love you both so very much.

Some of the events, names and identifying details
Have been changed to protect the privacy of individuals.
Some events have been compressed and some dialogue
has been recreated to protect the innocent.

Contents

Forward

"Suddenly" is a must read by every woman. Exposing deceit and fraud under the disguise of love and showing us that wolves in sheep's clothing are very much still alive.

Ada Madison is truly a survivor having overcome many life circumstances. But nothing could have prepared her for when she thought she had finally met the man of her dreams. She thought to herself, "Could such a wonderful man exist?" "Could he be the answer to my prayers?"

Little did she know that she was about to embark on a journey that would change the course of her life forever. From a successful businesswoman having it all to finding herself in a shelter years later.

So, where do you go when everything you knew has been left behind? You run to God who puts angels in your path.

Holding strong to her faith and trust in the Lord, Ada overcame the abusive emotional scars of a shattered life filled with shame and self-guilt and arose to a vibrant strong woman to tell her story bravely.

Today, Ada attends Champions City Church in Orlando, Florida and her passion is to warn and help other women who are still struggling with the scars and pain of an abusive and deceptive relationship.

Fear could have paralyzed her but we can truly say that Ada is a true champion in every sense of the word.

Pastors Alexander and Sandra Sarraga
Champions City Church, Orlando
www.championscitychurch.org

Acknowledgments

Above all, I thank my Abba and my Lord Jesus Christ, to whom I give all the glory, all the honor, and all the praise. Without His mercy I would not be alive today.

To my son, Julian Thomas, I thank God every day for you. I love you with all of my heart and am so very proud of you. I am blessed to call you my son.

To my dad, whom I love so very deeply, I thank you. When no one else remained, you loved me, encouraged me, and gave so generously of your love and care. Thank you, Dad. I have the best daddy in the world.

To Sally Duback, I love you and I thank you for igniting my creativity and loving me back to life.

To John Ramirez, I thank you for your prayers, encouragement, generosity, and words of wisdom. You have greatly impacted my life and changed it forever.

Apostles Alexander and Sandra Sarraga, I love you guys. I will be forever grateful for your love, mentoring, guidance, care, prayers, and your encouragement. It was your push and encouragement, John and

Apostles Alexander and Sandra, that made this book a reality. The three of you helped me to understand God's plan for my life.

To every person who reads this book, I pray God's healing flows through my story and gives you hope where there is hopelessness. I pray that like me, the mighty hand of God touches your heart and ignites His spirit in you.

Introduction

All my life, I never imagined that I would be writing this book. I thought the unthinkable could never happen to a woman like me. After all, how could it? I had worked hard as a young girl to not only find my way but to find success in my career, businesses, and life. The truth is that no one is immune. You never know where or when the wolf will show up in disguise.

It's not by accident, coincidence, or serendipity that you are about to read my story; a divine appointment has led you to hold this book in your hands. The facts you are about to read are disturbing and hard to believe, but true.

Every day in the United States, women are murdered at the hands of their husband or male partner. Between 2001 and 2012, 6,488 American troops lost their lives in Afghanistan. During that same time, 11,766 American women were murdered by their current or ex male partners, right here in the US. That is nearly double the casualties lost during the war. Three women are murdered daily by their current or former male partner. Every single minute in the US, twenty women are victims of intimate partner violence. On average there are more than 20,000 domestic violence calls daily. One in five women will be raped, 46.7 percent of them by someone they know and 29 percent of them by an intimate partner. Additionally, 19.3 million women are stalked in their lifetime, 43 percent of them by former partners. Financial abuse happens in most all domestic abuse cases either by theft, manipulation, or fear of complete lack.

Sociopaths love online dating. It is like a haven for them, and you are fooling yourself if you believe background checks are performed. Unfortunately, anyone can create an online profile and become your greatest fantasy come true. Even the "safest" of sites can be easily manipulated.

We've all heard stories of meeting someone who looked twenty years older than their profile picture. But what if it were far more serious than that? What if you are confronted with the wolf dressed in fine sheep apparel? If there were a box to check on the profile builder that said rapist, thief, murderer, batterer, abuser, sadist, or sociopath, I would
venture to say it would always be left blank. If this book doesn't speak to you now, it will at least help protect you or someone you love from an unsuspecting wolf in disguise. As hard as it is to see in black and white, one in two women reading this will be assaulted.

This book needs to be shared with every woman and their partners, young or old, married or single. May my transparency—and the courage God has given me to share it—bring hope, healing, and awareness of the wolf that lurks at every woman's door. This is my story.
Ada Madison

Part One: Once upon a time…

Iowa Girl

Although I'm a girl from Iowa, my childhood was not as "Norman Rockwell" as you might assume. Although her people are kind, hardworking, and honest, I learned that Iowa is a really good place to be *from*.

I am the firstborn of five and the only girl in my family. Dave came next and then Tommy. My parents told me not to play with my friend Reneé because she was sick. She didn't seem sick when we played on the swings one afternoon. She gave me rubella, German measles. I gave them to my pregnant mother. Tommy was born with a severely underdeveloped heart. He was the sweetest, happiest baby brother. I loved Tommy and how he lit up when I played with him. When Mom fed him his morning cereal, I would stick my tongue out and blow hard, making all sorts of noise. My baby brother would pull his knees up and explode with laughter, spitting his food all over the place. Mom and I laughed right along with him. I was Mom's helper with my two baby brothers.

One day, when Tommy was only a few months old, everything in our world changed. I watched Thomas Madison die in my mother's arms. I didn't understand death, but I saw and felt unmatchable pain when Tommy passed. From that moment on, everything changed. It even seemed like the sun did not shine as bright as it once had. The laughter in our home grew silent, and I would hear Mom crying at night when I was in bed.

My brave mother carried on with a beautiful smile and had two more boys, Michael and Joseph, over the course of the next few years. Dad worked hard and many times was only home on the weekends. Our home was busy with not only my brothers but also with Mom babysitting Scotty. Scotty's mom worked in an office downtown. She wore bright red lipstick and skirts with high heels. I would sit with my chin in my hands and stare at her in admiration from the breakfast table as she dropped Scotty off every morning. At night when she picked him up, that bright red lipstick was still there. I dreamed of wearing that same lipstick, skirt, and high heels.

I spent a lot of time with all of my grandparents. Only as an adult did I realize that they were from opposite sides of the tracks. Dad's parents, "Grampa" Ole and "Gramma" Ada, were the warmest, happiest, most fun-loving people. Grampa ran as he gave me rides on his shoulders around the neighborhood. He made me feel like the most beautiful and adored little girl in the world. When he came home from work at the factory, he would go straight to the shower. Fresh out of the bathroom, he'd have his hair slicked back, a fresh shave, and would reach down and scoop me up. I can still smell his Old Spice aftershave and feel how strong his arms and hands were as he held me. Oh how I loved my Grampa.

Gramma was a tiny, little thing with a great big giggle and a constant huge smile. I would stand on her feet, and she would dance the jitterbug to big band music all over her living room as I hung on for the ride. Sometimes I went to work with my Gramma Ada. She managed a bar inside a bowling alley near her home. I thought I was the cat's meow sitting up on that barstool, in that dimly lit bar, sipping kiddie cocktails with extra cherries at the bottom of a fancy glass. I knew all of her regulars, and they knew me by name. Evie worked with my Gramma and always brought in a new

set of ribbons to tie huge bows on my pigtails. Life was fun with Gramma Ada and Grampa Ole.

Moms' dad, Fred, is my "Gramp." Early in his legal career, Gramp started an insurance company. He was brilliant, persnickety, and drove a big Oldsmobile convertible. He would pick my brothers and me up on Sunday afternoons with the top down and take us to Baskin-Robbins for ice cream. I would wait all week for that joyous ride. My brothers would get a single dip and sit together in the backseat. I would get a triple dip and so would Gramp. I rode in the front with him, beaming like the queen of the parade. It never lasted too long though. Gramp would drive us back home immediately. He wanted the boys out of his car fast so they could finish their cones outside. In his trunk, he'd stored pre-wet towels and cleaning supplies to clean his car. That was my Gramp, persnickety.

My "Gram" Bobbie, like Gramp, was also a college graduate. Gram

18

was an artist, an activist for women's rights, and an amazing gourmet cook. My Gram would take me to the Art Center, where I would

watch her create. One day, Gram gave me a huge surprise: Instead of just watching, I'd be starting art camp for the summer. I loved it and found out I was a lot better at art than ballet. Gram had been taking me to all sorts of "lessons" that year. She had me in ballet, tumbling, tap dance, piano, and baton lessons. I excelled only in the tutus and bright red lipstick that I proudly paraded around in at all the recitals.

Early on, I learned that I lacked rhythm and coordination and had just about no athletic ability. But I also learned that I could strut my stuff in bright red lipstick and tackle just about anything creative. Gram told me that not every girl could draw the way I did. Gram also told me that not every girl could wear bright red lipstick quite the way I did. I loved my Gram. As she exposed me to the finer things in life, we had so much fun.

The last memory I have of Gram and me alone was the day we saw Rudolf Nureyev and Mikhail Baryshnikov in performance. I wore a shiny pink dress, and Gram had a new, bright pink lipstick for me hidden in her purse. When we got into her car, she let me put it on. I saw tears streaming down Gram's face as we watched those two men dance in tights on that huge stage. I didn't understand why, but I was moved too—by the dance, the stage, the sound, the lights—and I joined her. Gram and I cried as we watched that ballet together.

"Gramma Mad," Ruth Madison, was the matriarch of our family and much like her daughter, Gram. Gramma Mad was strong, hardworking, and fiercely independent. She was an entrepreneur most of her life. Gramma Mad was an extremely talented seamstress and clothing designer. I spent quite a bit of time with her. She taught me manners, how to listen to opera without giggling, how to walk in her high heels, and how to dig in the mud. I loved all of my grandparents. They were the glue in our family.

I spent my days at St. Augustine's Catholic School wishing I was anywhere else. I would watch the clock, waiting for the three o'clock bell to freedom. It's funny because I have no memory of Jesus or God ever being discussed at home. Sister Maria talked about Jesus and God all the time. She also ruled her second grade classroom with the whack of a wooden map pointer. She sneered at me every morning as I stifled my skip and shuffled in to take my seat.

Sister Maria loved to humiliate me and seemed to delight in punishing me. My class had a game that we loved to play. As quietly as we could, we would pass a little note around the room. One at a time, row to row, each one of us would write "Hi" on the note and pass it to the desk in front of us. My desk sat at the front of my row and directly in front of Sister Maria's desk. Every time I would reach to pass that little note across the aisle, it seemed that Sister Maria would whirl around and point her long, crooked finger at me and summon me to the front of the room. Giggles would erupt from my classmates, and I always had this pit in my tummy, this dread of knowing what was coming.

Sister Maria would draw a tiny little "x" on the blackboard and tell me to hold my hands behind my back and put my nose on it. To do this, I had to stand on my tippy toes. I knew my freckled nose would be white with chalk dust and so did she. I would imagine my class pointing and laughing at me. No matter how hard I tried, it never took that long before my legs would get wobbly and shake. As much as I hated it, eventually I would drop my heels down and my nose would come off the "x." There she would be, waiting. Whack! The back of my legs would sting when Sister Maria's wooden map pointer lashed against my calves. I felt humiliated as my attempts to stifle my tears failed. Sister Maria didn't like me, and I didn't like her. I didn't know the word "hypocrite" yet, but in my heart I knew that's what she was. I didn't want to get into more trouble, so I never told my mother.

One day, Mom noticed the marks on my legs and asked me what had happened. I explained honestly. She looked surprised and told me I could go outside to play. The next day at school, it happened again. I was standing in front of the whole class feeling total humiliation as that nun wailed on my legs. Just then, Dad walked into my classroom. The class gasped as I turned and saw Dad. I wasn't sure if I would be in even greater trouble or if he was there to rescue me. Dad told me to get my things—all my things. Dad took me out for ice cream before driving us home. I never went back to that Catholic place again.

In my fifth grade year, near Thanksgiving, my parents announced that we were moving from Des Moines back to Cedar Rapids. I had lived in Cedar Rapids as a very young girl but felt Des Moines was my "home" now. The thought of leaving my school and friends and beloved grandparents saddened me deeply. We also learned that Mom had decided to return to college. As we pulled out of that long driveway, my brothers and I waving from the backseat of our station wagon, I thought my life was over. I waved goodbye to Gram, Gramp, Gramma Mad, and my best friend and cried myself to sleep. I woke up excited to be back in the same town as my Gramma Ada and Grampa Ole.

Starting fifth grade in a new school in the middle of the year was hard. That awkward yet familiar feeling of being a misfit engulfed me again. Soon the shelter of innocence began to disappear when I stepped foot into junior high. One day, Mom offered to pay me five dollars if I lost five pounds. That was the first time I noticed I was fat. I developed horrible feelings about my body. I cried myself to sleep many, many nights as I wished I could go back to being who I had been when I was a little girl in Des Moines. Junior high overwhelmed me.

In our school, we had our own smoking lounge. It made us feel grown up smoking Marlboro Reds and blowing smoke rings at recess. That same school year, my friends and I discovered marijuana. It seemed that everyone smoked something. The teachers turned a blind eye to it all, and, in fact, one of our teachers supplied us with all the marijuana we wanted. My twelve-year-old world grew more isolated and much darker. I cried myself to sleep most nights and felt very alone. Life was so different than it had been in Des Moines.

I was in trouble a lot at home. Mom and Dad told me I was rebellious. I didn't feel like a rebel. I felt misunderstood and unloved. At age thirteen, I started running away from home. I felt like a failure and a disappointment to my parents. I felt fat, ugly, and ashamed. After our move from Des Moines, I was completely separated from my parents' and brothers' daily lives. It seemed impossible that things could ever be the same again. My brothers excelled in sports and school. Mom and Dad attended all their sporting events. It seemed I excelled at nothing. There was fishing trips and snowmobile outings and trips "for the boys" only. I always wondered why there was never a trip for the girl.

When I was sixteen, Mom broke her femur in a skiing accident and wound up in the hospital for months. She needed my help to keep our household going, and every day from her hospital bed, she instructed me about what to do. I did all of the grocery shopping, cooking, laundry, and even laid clothes out for my sweet colorblind dad. In the beginning, it was fun. I felt needed and important; however, my brothers became resentful of me and reminded me that I was not their mother. The chasm between my brothers and I grew. Dad was hurting, stressed out and missed Mom. I felt like no one in that house cared about me. I ran away for the final time that year. I left school that day too and never went back—three months away from graduating high school early.

I was accustomed to working and liked providing for myself. I had started my first job beyond babysitting when I was twelve, and now I looked forward to full-time work and complete independence. However, deep inside, I wished my family would run after me and tell me they wanted me home. I yearned to be like my brothers.

At seventeen, I met Scott and married him three months later. I thought Scott was fatherly, mature, and worldly, mostly because he shaved and was twenty. He said he was in love with me. I thought Scott would take care of me and love me forever. I was working in a factory and would rather die than spend the rest of my life there. With my ever-present love of lipstick and fashion, I dove into a cosmetology career and started attending cosmetology college. Quickly, I learned that cosmetology wasn't considered real college. Before I started Mom told me I was too smart to waste my time there. I needed to go to "real college," and she added that my grandparents would pay my tuition to a "real" college. I was set on proving myself, however, so I put myself through school. I constantly challenged and pushed myself to be the very best I could be. I was first in my class, student council president, and totally unfulfilled. I was ashamed of quitting high school and yearned for my family to be proud of me.

Before I finished school, I was blessed with an awesome job offer made by Liv, the most respected woman in our city. I worked very long hours in her upscale salon and was developing my clientele quickly. In addition to her salon, Liv also worked as an educator nationally. She was older than Mom and never had any children of her own. Liv immediately took me under her wing and taught me so much. I was like a sponge, soaking up everything she had to say. In the cosmetology industry, we refer to the hair gurus who wear a headset and wield shears on a stage, teaching crowds, as "platform artists." Liv was a platform artist with an international reputation as a groundbreaking visionary in the industry. I was thrilled to be learning from her, but I wanted more.

Besides developing my own clientele, I decided to spend twenty-five hours a week assisting Liv, free of charge. I cherished this apprenticeship. I didn't pay her and she didn't pay me; instead, we had a mutual agreement. I would learn from Liv and stand by her side, formulating her colors, discussing design concepts, sweeping hair from the floor, blow-drying and styling her guests. Gradually, Liv began standing back and watching me perform the services on her clients. She would sit on her stool, sipping her hot water as she watched me create. Her clients were the affluent of the city, and they tipped me very well.

Every day around five o'clock, when Liv's day was ending, my own clients would start coming in. I worked very long hours, but the education I was receiving was invaluable. After about six months, I was quickly going from hair sweeper and protégé to educating Liv's staff. My business had grown beyond what I could have ever dreamed. Many of my clients had been referred to me by Liv's elite clients who I had worked with as I assisted her. So there I was, busy and educating people old enough to be my parents and respected in that little world. But I felt empty at home. I wanted more.

One day, Liv asked me to travel with her and assist her on stage. I was thrilled at the proposition! I began styling and doing makeup and general assisting for Liv on the stage. I remember the rush of the first time. It was avant-garde fashion and design and everything I craved as a young designer. Music, lights, and a whole lot of fun filled this world. Soon Liv began asking me questions on stage and handed me the microphone. When an audience member would ask questions during the Q & A, Liv would hand me the mic. I felt like a nervous wreck, but to my surprise I looked calm and cool as a cucumber on the video footage. Liv told me I was a natural. Soon we were a team, and I had earned my own headset and chair to create in on stage. Now I too wielded shears before a crowd. I absolutely loved the rush of the audience, the stage, and the wild hair design we would create. Artistically, it was unmatched by anything my Iowa clientele would ever allow me to do.

I enrolled in the University of Northern Iowa for a microteaching course that would allow me the license to teach on my own. After I passed those boards, one gig led to another and I was off and running.

I was a successful cosmetologist with a great following. Also, I had a teaching sideline that allowed me to travel to some great shows and to teach continued education at the area community colleges—all of this and I was barely into my twenties. This led to studying and taking the exam for the prestigious educational and design team for the National Cosmetology Association. I studied for a month and walked in prepared. Little did I know I'd be almost the youngest there by over a decade. I did it. I was in! It was fun and allowed me to meet many industry greats from around the US. But it wasn't enough. I was empty inside. I wanted more.

The competition arena fascinated me, and I was young enough to have no fear. Liv pushed me to go for it, and I did. Hairstyling competitions are crazy artistic fun. It is technical and extremely precise but has a profound artistic freedom and an edge to it. It was a perfect match for my inner artist and youthful energy. Preparing for a competition took hundreds of hours. My long days now stretched to midnight most nights of the week and all day Sundays as I prepared my model, technique, form, and timing. It all had to be perfect and complete in minutes to be even considered in the running. To my excitement, I placed in the very first show I entered. The stage, the trophy, and the press were thrilling for this young girl from Iowa. I competed all over the place, and soon my little area of the salon looked like a bowling alley with all the trophies, medals, and plaques. But that was not enough. I still felt empty and unnoticed by anyone I loved. I wanted more.

At the end of the year, I vacationed in Florida and saw the Gulf of Mexico for the first time. The beach was awesome with its white sand, palm trees, and clear blue water; but what really got my attention was the hair. There was glaring opportunity for a good designer there. Before that week ended, Scott and I decided to move to Florida. Four weeks later, we were on our way with Liv cheering me on. I had a pit in my stomach but huge excitement and joy as I waved goodbye to my family gathered in the picture window of that little ranch house. I pulled away, and as I hit the highway I looked at Iowa in my rearview mirror and felt like the chains of confinement and smallness were broken. Soon I would be starting over in Naples, Florida. I was excited to put my toes in the warm, white sandy beaches of that chic and cosmopolitan city on the Gulf of Mexico. Yes, Iowa was a good place to be *from*.

White Sand, Blue Water,

& New Beginnings

There were no cell phones in those days, and the drive from Iowa to Florida seemed like a journey to China. I followed Scott in my car, and he drove the moving truck packed tightly with all of our belongings mile after mile until finally we arrived in Naples. Life began to happen quickly in Florida as we hurried to empty the moving truck and start our new life. Scott and I had hoped that our new start would breathe life into our almost nonexistent marriage, but it didn't. Soon after we arrived, we peacefully finalized our failed attempt at happily ever after.

I immediately went to work, built an affluent clientele, bought a condo, and had the financial ability to go and do most anything I wanted to. I also quickly fell in love with a beautiful Hispanic man, Justo. Justo would become my next husband and father to my only child. Justo was separated and in the process of a divorce when he found out that his soon to be ex-wife was pregnant with their only child. Our relationship began as a great friendship. I was Justo's confidant and he was mine.

Justo and I spent hours discussing our failed marriages. We fell in love and married two years later. I loved Justo more than I ever imagined was possible. I knew he would care for me and I would care for him for the rest of our lives. I was positive that "happily ever after" was forever with Justo. I adored that man. I also loved my new role as wife and stepmommy to his baby girl, Justine. Justine and I were best of friends and spent hours and hours reading books, making cookies, painting nails, curling hair, dressing up, coloring, and playing together. She was my little princess.

When we learned I was pregnant, we were over-the-top excited. Less than ten months after we were married, our son, Julian, was born. My pregnancy was active, happy, and fun. I enjoyed every single second, every move he made, and every kick I felt as my baby grew inside of me. I awakened one morning with cramps and decided to go for a long walk along the water. About fifteen minutes into my walk, those cramps worsened. As I turned back for home, I realized I was in labor. Excitement filled me as the anticipation of meeting my baby drew near. In my heart, I knew he was a boy.

As we raced to the hospital, Justo and I were still talking about names. We were deeply in love and extremely excited to meet our baby. We discussed names while we nervously waited for the traffic lights to turn green. At the hospital, they checked me into a room and the cramps intensified. I practiced the techniques I had learned in Lamaze class and grew more and more excited.

After almost eighteen hours, my doctor told me I had not dilated at all.

They gave me a drug through an IV to move things along. The pain intensified, and the contractions grew closer, but I still was not dilating. After thirty-six hours of labor, the unthinkable suddenly happened: My baby's heart stopped! And mine did too. The fetal monitor squealed an emergency call as the doctor raced into my room. To this day, I have never experienced the fear I felt as they ran pushing me in my bed from labor to delivery. The doctor and a handful of nurses ran and pulled me in that bed with an IV in my arm as they raced down that hallway toward the elevator.

I looked into Justo's fearful face. Confusion seemed to hover over us as the doctor shouted orders to nurses. They were running toward the elevator as the doors opened. My bed crashed into the back of the elevator wall as we entered. My head hit the wall and a goose egg immediately appeared, but that paled in comparison to my fear. The doctor and nurses spoke to each other over me as if I were not there. I heard phrases like "permanent brain damage," and terror filled my heart. The doctor shouted to the nurses, "Take the stairs and clear the room. There's no time for prep. This child needs oxygen now!" The nurses obeyed quickly and were there waiting as the doctor raced my bed into the room.

From an operating table, a young pregnant woman with her husband looked over her shoulder at me. She was draped for an obviously planned C-section, and her doctor had just begun her surgery. My doctor yelled, "Clear the room now. Emergency!" as he placed a mask over my face. I cried out to God. I asked God to please protect my baby and guide the doctor's hands. I breathed in the anesthesia from the mask as I looked over at that young couple. Their shocked faces were the last thing I remembered before waking up.

I heard myself scream in a panic as I awoke in a cold recovery room, startling the nurse that stood beside me. She took my hand and quickly assured me that my eight-pound, eight-ounce baby boy was in perfect health. I began to cry, and soon Justo was by my side with joy and pride and a love that I had never seen from him. He kissed my forehead and told me he was proud of me. At that moment, I fell even deeper in love with him.

Justo laughed as I tried to get a detailed description of our baby's looks. Soon, the nurse was wheeling me to a room with the promise of bringing my baby to meet his mommy. Suddenly, another nurse came from behind us and laid Julian in my arms on that rolling bed. My heart leaped with pure joy. When I held our baby, I felt like my heart was going to explode. Instant tears of gratitude and love overcame every cell of my body. Tears fell, and the most indescribable and incredible love washed over me as my sweet little baby boy stared deeply into my eyes and smiled.

I was Julian's mommy. He had big, dark brown eyes and a thick head of black, wavy hair. I told Julian I loved him, and I thanked God for him as I kissed his sweet little pouty lips. Julian was the most perfect, beautiful baby I had ever seen. He was so smart and alert. He took in everything that happened around him. I fell in love over and over again as I fed him and he focused on my face, cooing away. He melted me into a mushy, happy ball of the greatest joy I have ever known. I had been given a miracle, and I knew it. All I could do was cry. I was so overcome with joy and thankfulness and the most amazing love that I had ever known.

For the first time in my life, I felt I had a real purpose: I was Julian's mommy, Justine's stepmommy, and Justo's wife. When I looked into Julian's eyes, I felt unconditionally loved. He was pure joy and so was Justine. Although I did not give birth to her, I had known Justine since she was an infant and I loved her deeply. I worried that she'd feel left out when her baby brother came home. Justine and I had practiced how she would hold the wipes and help me change her brother's diaper. I wanted her to feel needed from day one of his life.

I dreamed of Justine and Julian being very close all their lives. I wanted them to have the love for each other that I had always wished my brothers had for me. I adored my little princess as if she were my own. Justine grew up knowing that she was never in my tummy but always in my heart. Soon after we brought Julian home, Justine went from calling me "A-duhhh" to "Mommy." I was deeply touched when she shyly called me Mommy the first time with a look that almost asked my permission to do so. I told her I loved her so much and that I was very proud and honored to be called Mommy.

Not long afterward, Justine was in the awkward position of not knowing what to call me when her biological mommy and I were present at the same time. It broke my heart to see that little one struggle. When her mom left, we did Justine's favorite thing: we made no-bake cookies together and cut them into bars. We had a heart-to-heart talk over her favorite Minnie Mouse cup filled with milk and a still-warm-cookie bar on her big brass bed. Those huge brown eyes on my three-year-old princess would melt your heart. I told Justine that she was my first child and my baby girl and nothing would ever change that. Justine's eyes grew big when I told her she could call me anything she wanted to and that names did not matter. She was a huge fan of Peter Pan books and movies, and without thinking I said, "You could even call me Peter Pan!" Justine giggled until I thought we would both wet our pants. From that day on I was "Mommy" unless her mother was with us, and then I was "Pete." It was our special secret. Julian and Justine and their dad were the center of my world. I wanted my kids to have everything that I never had. I was determined to be the best mother and wife I knew how to be.

Not long after I arrived in Florida, I had opened the doors to my first salon, Ada & co. My business prospered and grew very quickly. Soon, I was a sought-after high-end stylist with a six-month waiting list. That business success provided well for our family. We lived in a beautiful home with a pool, a hot tub, and huge veranda for family fun and business parties. That gorgeous home was in an upscale, highly desirable family neighborhood, nestled in on a lake with a beautifully landscaped, wooded lawn. Our backyard featured a stilted clubhouse and swing set. Like a magnet, our home drew neighbors and all of the kids' friends. So there I was, a girl from Iowa, living in deep gratitude

34

beyond what I had ever imagined possible. I had a precious, happy, and joyful son, a beautiful stepdaughter I adored, and a handsome, charming husband.

Shortly after Julian's birth, Justo decided to stay home and go to college. I encouraged him and cheered him on as he went after his dreams of a career in medicine. I was happy that Julian and Justine's father would be there with them after school. This would allow me to work long hours. Justo attended several schools before he decided on the career path he wanted to follow. I continued to grow my business, which provided lavishly for all of us.

Life was full and very happy, but the demands of business alongside the joys of motherhood were hard and sometimes exhausting. I was the homeroom mom, the art volunteer, the treat baker, the slumber party mom, the team mom, the PTA mom, and I never missed a game, activity, or event. At the same time, I grew and mentored a team of salon and spa professionals in my business five to six days a week, and on the seventh day, I did inventory, payroll, and accounting, and ordered supplies. I loved every minute of this seven-day-a-week juggling act. By outside standards, I had it all. But at home, my marriage was slipping.

Justo was growing distant and seemed indifferent about his career goals. Oftentimes, he would go many months without attending school. He seemed content that I was the sole provider. I grew resentful and felt he didn't appreciate me. In anger, I lashed out at

Justo, but inside I desperately wanted him to love and provide for me. He just grew more distant. Justo sat back completely, and I ran the show. In doing so, I felt terrible about myself. Deep inside, I wanted Justo to lead our family. The thought became almost laughable. It seemed my strength in business steamrolled over Justo's manhood. He was content to let me wear the pants. I made matters worse by lobbing verbal putdowns at him. I hated his lack of care or motivation, and I hated myself for acting the way I did. I desperately wanted to be led by a man who loved me. I hid my feelings from everyone, including Justo, most of the time. I kept smiling and working and being Mom.

My relationship with my own mom and dad had been growing beyond anything I ever could have imagined the day I left Iowa. Mom had become my closest friend. She and Dad absolutely adored Julian, and loved Justine just as if she were their own. As our friendship deepened, Mom began confiding in me about everything. This made me feel like I was part of the family even though I was so far away. But with our closeness came the unveiling of a family that was not as clean on the inside as I had always thought. I learned the depth of some of my family members' addictions. Addictions and depression seemed to be like an embarrassing uncle that was always just brushed under the rug or stashed in the closet of denial.

Justo's and my life in Florida was on autopilot when a sudden explosion changed everything forever. Julian, Justine, and I flew to my parents' home for a few days of fun, and then I returned alone to

Florida. For the first time, the kids were staying without me, with Gramma, Grampa, and their cousins in Wisconsin. They would have two action-packed weeks of fun before I joined them for one last week. It was an awesome vacation for all of us. A few days after we all returned home together, our worlds came crashing down in a way that none of us could have ever imagined. Justo was angry. He approached me to say that Justine's mother had called and said she had decided not to return—ever. I just looked at him stunned and not understanding his words.

Justo informed me that Justine had told her mother we had been abusive to her and that she never wanted to return. I could not begin to process the lie or where it came from. My heart split in two for Justo, Julian, and myself. Justine was only twelve years old and a tremendous joy in our lives. After a month of no contact, unthinkable pain, and confusion, my parents flew down. They talked to Justine's mother and arranged to take Justine to the beach. I remember waiting for their return, looking out our front window. My heart pounded as I saw Mom's sad face as they pulled back into the driveway. Mom cried and said it was as if Justine was a completely different little girl.

Months went by, and Justo was not even allowed to speak to her. I would bake her favorite things and have them waiting on the counter in hopes that the nightmare was about to end and Justine would come dancing through the door. I bought her clothes I knew she would love and had them waiting on her bed with matching nail polish, just like always. That month stretched into two. Julian was only nine and was heartbroken. Like all of us, he did not understand what was going on. Soon Thanksgiving came and went, and an empty place loomed in our home and in our hearts. Christmas came and went with many silent tears.

Julian grew mad at his sister. His birthday came and went, and soon the school year was coming to an end. I was on autopilot at work and home as I tried to hold things together for Julian. My heart was shattering for him, Justo, and myself. It felt like a death that we could not mourn. At the same time, Justo pulled farther and farther away from me. Betrayal and heartbreak filled every crevice of my heart and soul. After a year of watching my son's heartbreak over the sudden loss of his sister and trying to keep my own broken heart in check, I made the decision that would surely fulfill my heart's desires for Julian: We would sell our home and my business and relocate to Milwaukee, where my parents and one of my brothers' families now lived. Julian was excited to be moving to his grandparents and beloved cousin and "brother" Dave's town. Our home and my business sold quickly.

In those days, I turned to God only when I needed Him. I placed 911 calls to God in emergency scenarios or reached for Him like the aspirin on the top shelf of the medicine cabinet. He never let me down. I had felt nudged by God to go "home." As I pulled out of my driveway in Florida, intense pain seared my heart. I wondered if I would ever see my baby girl again. I wondered if our marriage would survive. Never in my wildest imagination could I have dreamed of what lay ahead.

Coming Home

I remember the night we purchased our home on the Internet, sight unseen. A cute, well-kept alley separated our yard from my parents' place. The day I left Iowa I could never have imagined that I'd return to nest in my parents' backyard. We all were excited about this change. It took the focus off the raw wound left by Justine's sudden disappearance.

Our new home was a fantastic little stone house with sidewalks and a canopy of huge trees that lined the street. It was nestled in a quaint, artsy, affluent, and historic village on the North Shore of Milwaukee. Julian was having a ball with his grandparents and cousin Dave. I looked forward to taking as much time off as I needed before diving into another business.

While our new home was beautiful, our marriage was crumbling. Justo and I tried counseling, but it was too late. We had both erected walls in our minds that seemed insurmountable. Our happily ever after ended. It was painful and left a deep sense of failure in my heart. Despite everything, Julian thrived. He was the joy and the love of my life.

That small North Shore suburb was like a small town out of a storybook. Julian could skate downtown to the candy store only a couple blocks away from our home and walk just about anywhere. He was safe, and most of the other families in the community had two parents and houses full of love. I felt good about bringing Julian to Wisconsin. His broken heart over Justine, followed by my divorce from his dad, were softened by having his beloved grandparents right in his backyard.

Julian and Mom's closeness continued to grow into amazing levels of love, adoration, and a deep sense of the true family that my son and I craved. They talked about everything. It was healing to watch, and their bond gave me such hope. It also healed some of my childhood wounds that had lain buried deep in my heart.

With my mother's encouragement, I dove into art. I met an artist named Jo and spent a lot of time at her studio creating art with a group of women who soon became great friends. One day as I returned home from the studio, I passed a
newly erected "for rent" sign on a gorgeous, historic stone building, and I turned into its parking lot. Within two hours, I negotiated and signed a lease and was officially off and running again—this time in a three-story property. For the first time in all my years of business, Mom helped me "set up shop." We had the time of our lives together preparing for the grand opening.

The main floor featured an expansive line of salon and spa products, a makeup studio, and a huge "Gift Art Gallery." I carried art for the home inside and out, jewelry, and wearable art from all over the world. We branded ourselves as the funky, artfully unique place to shop.

Everything was wrapped and packaged in an unforgettable way. In the gallery, objects hung from ceilings, glassed-in antique deep-window displays, and ultramodern glass displays. It was a juxtaposition of historic and state-of-the-art modern decor. Deep purple high-gloss tile floors bumped up to original wooden floors from 1869. The salon was just off of the gallery, overlooking trees and water. An open staircase led to the lower walkout level for spa nail services and offices. The top floor featured the spa offering abundant services in an extremely peaceful environment. That place married many years of experience with salon, art, and retail under one roof. It was a dream realized . . . a dream that would be clouded by devastating news that would change the course of our lives.

When the Unthinkable Happened

I wondered if anyone else noticed her dry cough. It was just a little dry cough, but it hadn't stopped in weeks. Mom was tiny, athletic, with big brown eyes and dark hair framing her gorgeous face. She was the picture of health. She attributed that cough to a desert vacation.

I insisted that Mom go to the doctor. During his meeting with her, he immediately became suspicious. Her doctor ordered an X-ray, which led to a biopsy. After her biopsy, the doctor came out to speak with Dad and me without Mom present. The waiting room was a large open atrium with an open staircase in the center that led to the main entrance. I looked up to see the doctor striding quickly toward us with an emotionless face. Without a blink or single emotion he said, "It's lung cancer. It's aggressive, and it's too late. I'm sending her to an oncologist right away. Usually this type of cancer ends your life in thirty days to three months."

My father fell backward. He tripped and hit the wall behind him. I felt the room spin and my heart stop. I couldn't breathe. Without any emotion, the surgeon turned and walked away. People stopped and stared, and I felt as if a nuclear bomb had just exploded. I grabbed ahold of Dad and held him as he cried. Over and over, he said that he was sorry for me. Dad said he was so sorry that Mom and I would lose each other. He told me I was her best friend. This was the first step of the hardest time in my entire life.

I felt helpless to help those whom I loved. My heart was breaking over and over every day for Dad and Julian and my brave Mom. There was chemo and radiation. I have shaved many clients' heads as they've undergone chemo, but the day I shaved my precious Mom's head was different. She called me at work and asked me to bring my clippers home. Her doctor had told her almost down to the hour when to expect her hair to fall out. I learned from her that day that it hurt as it began to come out in clumps. Mom said every follicle was hurting.

That first time I shaved her head was the hardest haircut I've ever performed. It would be the first of many more times to come. We learned to have fun with it. One time, I left a little lock of curled hair on the crown of her head. We laughed and planned to have fun with Julian when he came home from school. It softened the blow of the "C" word for Julian and for all of us. Mom was always positive, always smiling, and always worrying about us.

I was attending church and shared everything I was learning with Mom. God seemed like a scary guy hiding behind a curtain, like the wizard of Oz to me. I would lay in bed at night, trying to pray. My Catholic roots had me mindlessly reciting "Our Father's," hoping to hear His voice. I hoped that I would learn more about Him though the new Bible study I had joined. I had an uneasy feeling and felt out of place, but I prayed that the women with the judgmental stares would give me a chance.

I would come to the study straight from work in my all-black attire. Black is not unique to the salon industry but rather the gold standard as a defense against staining hair colors. I was typically attired in black boots with a long black skirt and a whole lot of colorful jewelry. I felt like a misfit at that study. I would sit quietly among the Bible study group members and try to glean knowledge about God. I would share everything we discussed with Mom. Through that study I learned that Mom believed in Jesus. Jesus hadn't been discussed in our home when I was growing up. Two weeks into the study, I was asked to describe my world to the others. I used the words "chaos and sadness" to describe the fear I was walking in with Mom's cancer. I felt safe revealing my vulnerability because they were from church and believers, yet not a soul commented on what I had just said. They just stared at me with judgment. I didn't understand why. The next morning, the leader called me to ask that I meet with her at a local coffeehouse. I was excited and hoped maybe God was bringing a new friend.

At the coffeehouse, the leader immediately shocked me when she said she recognized cults because she'd been part of one. She told me it was obvious to everyone that I was a witch and that my entire black-clad staff was part of that dark world too. She stared at my shoes and said "combat boots" are not something any of the women in our group would wear. She told me to never come back and try to "infiltrate her group" again and added that a Christian would never use the word "chaos." She said they'd pray that I'd be saved before walking out.

I ran to my car in tears and went straight to Mom's. She was saddened but not surprised and shared how she'd always hated the harsh judgment and prejudice that surrounded religion. This study was a life group for one of the biggest and most affluent churches in our area. With Mom's prompting, I drove to the church and went straight into the lead pastor's office. I introduced myself and explained the reason for my visit. Very quickly it became apparent that he knew all about it. He explained that in a first-grade classroom, if one child is a disruption to the class, that child needs to be removed. He thought I was a witch too! I left his office knowing I did not have a church or a Bible study. As I cried my way home, I wondered why God had let this happen.

Having not found help at church, I decided on another route, I'd try to find Gee. To understand Gee I need to take you back to where we met and how I became entwined in what I would one day learn was a web of darkness. I met Gee in Florida many years before. She was a tarot card reader and a psychic who had frequented my Florida salon. Gee horrified me one day when she began predicting Mom's death from lung cancer, detail by detail as I colored her hair. I had just returned from a trip where my beloved Gramma Ada had died of lung cancer, holding my hand as she left this world. This had happened only a few days before Gee's awful prediction of Mom's death.

I explained to Gee that the details of her premonition were correct but not the person. She looked at me with a wild and distant stare as I explained my Gramma Ada's passing. Gee didn't acknowledge my words or even seem to register what I had said but instead responded with, "You're going to sell this business and move to a place with oak trees and snow. You will have a large building that will house your new business. It is your mother I am talking about." That was years before I would move to Milwaukee.

Looking at the snow and barren oak trees as I drove, I thought about that conversation long ago. With a little research I found Gee, and a long-distance friendship began. When I told her about Mom, she was not surprised. Gee said it would be years, not months, before she died. Gee prayed with me for Mom and spoke of Jesus, but something wasn't right with her. I didn't have the slightest idea that it was the occult, the devil himself, I was dabbling with.

Mom and Gee encouraged me to allow myself to think about love again. I spent all my free time with Julian and my parents. Inside I feared what I would do when Mom was gone. I couldn't bear to think of our world without her. I wondered how I would ever meet someone.

Dusk was a good friend and successful business owner, and she met a great guy online. Dusk told me that online dating was safe and that many people she knew had found their soulmate on the Internet. With many friends prompting, I decided to give it a whirl. Dusk and I devised a game plan that went like this: I would drive my car and meet my date at a specific and very expensive restaurant close to my house. If he hesitated at my suggestion of this restaurant, he would not be for me. I wasn't looking for men with money. I had my own. But I wasn't interested in a man looking for my money either. I was looking for a leader, a man to look up to.

Dusk and I also had an escape plan in place. The first guy was a successful high-profile lawyer. It was horrible from the start. Escape plan: I went to the ladies' room and called Dusk before returning to the table. Dusk called a few minutes later with an "emergency" that sent me rushing out apologizing to my date. Silly, but that is what we did. I screened my dates that way. Then one evening I met a really great man, Abel. I was impressed to learn about the Christian shelter for homeless men that he had built and the chapel it housed. He was very successful in business and an amazing musician. He was a strong man with a strong character and was sort of a bad boy but had a soft heart.

Abel's mother had passed away the year before. His father was a sweet, gentle giant whom I loved. Abel wined and dined me. We went to professional ballgames, theater, and amazing restaurants. We had a lot of fun, which distracted me from the pain at home. I only dated Abel when Julian was with Justo. Abel understood.

"Home" meant that Julian and I were with my parents; our home or theirs. That's how it was for a long time. When Mom started to get tired and I began to fear the end was near, Abel broke things off suddenly. I was hurt and shocked at the false accusations he'd made.

Mom really liked Abel. I believe she thought I'd marry him. I didn't tell her about our breakup. It was too painful to think of explaining another failure to her.

Mom taught me how to live and to embrace every day as if it was my last. There was love and laughter and lots of travel for my parents. They journeyed to New York City for the first time and had the time of their lives. They got their first passports and went to Italy for a month. They put almost a thousand miles on their snowmobiles that last winter. Mom's three months lasted three wonderful years. Then suddenly she was gone. Suddenly everything changed. Suddenly I couldn't do anything to ease the pain Julian and Dad were suffering. Suddenly nothing would ever be the same again.

Reflections from the Front Porch

I sat on Mom's porch and watched the ambulance drive away with her body. Just minutes before I had stood in her room alone, stoic and numb as they had gently lifted my precious mom from her bed. I had kept my hand on her and walked out with them and watched as they closed the door to the waiting ambulance. In the back of that vehicle lay my mothers body, and I would never see her again. Everything, including time, stood still. Complete silence, with the exception of the distinct sound of a singing cardinal, reigned. There he was, a bright red cardinal perched on the top of Mom's weather vane. That little guy was singing at the top of his lungs. I thought that signified that all of heaven was rejoicing as Mom went home. Her suffering was over.

I had the most profound feeling of empty, void loneliness that I've ever experienced. My heart felt like it was going to explode. My pain shifted to Julian. He was gone for the afternoon with his cousins. Many times over the course of the last three years, I'd thought about how and when she would leave. How was I going to tell Julian that his Gramma was gone? My heart absolutely shattered as I thought about the grief that lay ahead for Julian.

In my mind, our lives began to play out like a movie. I thought about the weeks leading up to this day. It had been so horrible and hard to watch my mother struggle. It was just as hard to watch my precious dad suffer helplessly.

The night before Mom's death, I'd brought her a colorful sculpture of an angel that I'd just completed. I hung it where she could see it from her bed. I called it *My Mother's Wings*. She had aked me to prop her up so she could see it better. When I did, she had whispered, "I love it, honey. It's beautiful." God and Mom gave me an incredible gift when she hugged me and uttered the last words she would say to me: "I love you, Ada, and I am so proud of you."

Mom had gently prepared us for that day, but I held her hand never wanting to let go. I watched her as she slept peacefully all night. Two big windows in that room offered views of her spectacular garden and works of her hands. It had been drizzling rain and gloomy for many days, which was very unusual for a Wisconsin July. The moment Mom took her last breath, it was like a giant florescent light suddenly flipped on. In a flash, a huge, bright light engulfed the room. The intensity of the moment had sent the hospice nurse running out in tears.

There's no possible way one could have experienced Mom's passing and not know for certain that God is real. God answered my prayer with that explosion of light. You see, Mom used to look at the beautiful wavy patterns on her floor that the light made as it streamed through her thick, wavy glass antique windows. Daily, the light made this beautiful display of art on her old wooden floors. She had told me that whenever I saw that light, I would know that she was there and that she was with God. I was grateful that God had brought that sudden burst of light into the room. But the truth is, I felt panicked. My best friend and only confidante was gone. I wasn't sure how I'd live without her.

My mind wandered as I stood there and I remembered that Gee had talked about a man I would meet right away after Mom ded. Gee said I would think that he wasn't "my type," and that initially, his voice and, specifically, his laugh would repel me. She also told me I was his soulmate and was destined to spend the rest of my life with him. Gee said he'd be a gift from God and that I wouldn't be alone for long. I wondered if I really was going to meet my soulmate soon. In a bizarre way, that thought gave me hope in that desperate moment of loss.

Autopilot

I felt like a lost little girl. I cried all the time with no control. Everywhere I went, everyone I saw, everything I did reminded me of Mom and the deep and gaping hole that now permanently resided in my heart. Walking through a grocery store could trigger a memory and like a floodgate opening, uncontrollable tears would flow. Tears came in the middle of a workday in the salon and at night as I tried to sleep. A sound or smell or the smallest thing would bring memories and rushing tears. The complete order and control I had always had over myself and my surroundings had vanished. I now knew grief in a very intimate way. When Mom left, a sense of being an orphan set into my soul.

I'd been preparing for a huge art show for many months before we lost Mom. She had loved being involved in the process. Now, I would be alone for this huge event and profoundly sad that Mom wasn't with me. I experienced critical acclaim at the show. My work reflected my beloved Mom's journey, including *My Mother's Wings*, the sculpture I had given her hours before she passed.

On opening night, I received a huge artistic flower arrangement. It was so large and extremely unique that it caught everyone's attention. I was surprised to learn it was for me. People gathered around me to ask whom it was from. I opened the card as they watched. The card read,

"I'm pulling for you, honey. I'm so proud of you and love you so very much. Mom." My heart was racing. I wanted to burst into tears. I wished I could lay my head on someone's shoulder at that moment, but I was alone. Then the circle of people started probing me again about the sender's identity. Is it Abel? they asked. I was afraid to open my mouth, believing that mere action would make me burst into tears. *Did Dad send them?* I wondered. For a moment, I also wondered if Mom had arranged this delivery before she died. I tried to act coy and told people it was a secret admirer. I walked outside and called Dad. It wasn't him, and Julian knew nothing about the flowers either. Several months later, the sender was revealed.

There was a man who had attended that show that evening who had asked lots of questions about me, friends told me later. A week after the show, he emailed me to say, "I knew that was you! I saw you at the art show." He'd noticed me online. His name was Damien. A few months later, I would learn Damien had sent those flowers and was there to watch me receive them.

A few days after Mom died, Abel had called with extreme remorse. He said he wanted to grow old with me, to spend the rest of his life with me. I was hurt, so I refused to see him. I had lost trust in him. I had believed he was the rock I'd been searching for. I now realize that I was simply desperate for love from a strong man who could lead. So I jumped into another relationship with Damien without even knowing it was happening. I desperately wanted to be loved. The security I felt to move forward with Damien had been planted years before. Gee was the gardener.

I was on a path straight to hell.

Prince Charming

Gee had called within minutes of Mom's death. How had she known Mom was gone? When Gee spoke, I experienced chills. A dark and very uncomfortable feeling engulfed me as I listened to her, unable to respond. Was Gee reading my mind?

Gee reminded me of the conversation we'd had about Mom many years before in Florida. She reminded me how she'd seen my mom's death and the move I would make to the Midwest. Then she reminded me of the man she had said I was going to meet very soon, the one she said I would feel wasn't my type and whose voice, specifically his laugh, would initially repel me. Gee had said he was my soulmate and that I was destined to spend the rest of my life with him. Six weeks later, I heard that horrible laugh—Damien. The curiosity lured me.

Damien's introduction began with an email after the art show and would lead to a romance that was like nothing I'd ever experienced. Damien was everything I ever dreamed of. However, he looked far different than any other man who had ever caught my attention. But before I would meet him in person, in our email exchanges and phone calls he revealed that he had been interested in me for quite a while. Damien told me he had been "checking me out" at my business and art shows. He said he'd learned of Mom's death and didn't want to interfere at such a difficult time. Damien divulged that he'd been at my art opening. He asked if I enjoyed the flowers he knew my mother would have sent! Damien had sent the flowers and attended the show to see my surprise.

Damien's gesture was bizarre given that we'd never met. I was shocked and confused. I didn't say a word, but Damien quickly took the lead. He told me he "prayed" that he wasn't out of line by sending flowers. He went on to tell me how he'd lost his father the year before and understood my pain. Although I had yet to meet him in person, he was charming and thoughtful. Damien was an impeccable gentleman on the phone and in emails. He continued to be extremely extravagant with the flowers he sent to me at the salon. His emails distracted me from terrible grief. Damien kept me busy when Julian was with Justo. I found myself emailing Damien and getting to know him over the phone even more.

After a few weeks, I agreed to meet Damien for dinner. Unlike anyone else, when I suggested our first-date restaurant, he took the lead immediately. Damien said it was one of his favorite places. He asked if we could go to lunch first, followed by a new exhibit at the art museum downtown, and then dinner at my go-to place. I met him for lunch, my escape plan in place. It was interesting that he loved art and chose the museum as a first meeting.

I was not physically attracted to Damien in the least, however, and his laugh completely repelled me. It was worse in person than it was on the phone. That sounds strange, but it is the truth. I literally could not stand the sound of that man's laugh. But I kept remembering what Gee had said. Unlike me, Damien seemed smitten with me from the first moment we met. He just stared at me a lot and told me I was a beautiful woman. He loved my hair. He loved my attire. He loved my shoes. He loved my perfume and on and on. As gushy as that sounds, his words seemed very genuine and soothed my weary heart. I didn't feel beautiful, but it was as if I had somehow dazzled him.

While I was not attracted to Damien, his continued, extravagant pursuit of me made me wonder if God had put him in my life. So I started to see Damien regularly. He was always a total gentleman—and extravagant! He showered me with gifts, flowers, expensive meals out, the theater, and surprise huge gift certificates waiting for me at my favorite boutique. My staff called him "the florist" because of the regular parade of wild, artsy flower arrangements that arrived at the salon.

Damien seemed to be getting serious very fast. This made me uncomfortable, but it also gave me a sense of security. His questions about my life made me feel he was safe, wholesome, old-fashioned, fatherly and honest. Damien seemed to have deep Christian values and standards. I admired that. It was important to him that I shared his Christian beliefs and values. That was new to me, and it felt safe and comfortable.

Damien couldn't wait for me to meet his family. He kept telling me how they were going to love me. Every single one of them was kind, loving, and superaccepting of me. They all seemed to genuinely like me and always wanted to include Julian and me in everything they did. They asked about my mom in a caring, understanding, and very loving way. I felt his family unconditionally accepted, loved, and respected me. Damien had two married kids, a son in college, four sisters and their families, and his mother.

I had always dreamed of having a sister, and now I quickly was being accepted as a "sister" by all four of his. One of them, Lind, and her mother, Dorothy, were artists. I loved that and felt an immediate connection to them. They all loved God and knew so much more spiritually than I did. I learned from them, and they slowly filled a huge, gaping void in my life that had existed since I was young. This superloving family softened the hole in my heart from divorce, the loss of Justine, the family I didn't have, and the loss of Mom. Somehow, Damien grew more attractive and I didn't hear that laugh any longer.

Damien adored Julian and Dad. He spoke about them all the time. He'd been blessed with tremendous success in business and was a natural, almost fatherly mentor to me. I trusted him. Within six months, he proposed to me with a big diamond ring. Damien had Julian, Dad, his kids, mother, sisters and even my dog involved in planning the proposal moment and buying the ring.

It was a bitter, cold Friday night, and I was finishing up after a very busy day at my salon. Julian was spending the night with Justo. It was cold, snowy, and about eight p.m. when I finally left the salon and trudged through the parking lot toward my car. The snow removal guys had plowed me in at the back of that lot, and I was dreading digging out my car in the cold. Lo and behold, my car was cleared out, and all the windows scraped. But there was more: a bouquet of flowers sat on the driver's seat. It was from Damien.

Damien had wanted to go for dinner downtown, but I had declined. I had told him the business was swamped and I needed to be there. Damien lived about forty-five minutes away. I thought about how he'd driven all that way to clear my car and leave that sweet card and flowers on my seat. I looked around thinking maybe he was somewhere in the parking lot, but he was nowhere in sight. That's how Damien was: over-the-top sweet.

I drove home and entered my cool little stone house from the back. I pulled into the garage and ascended a few stairs into the breezeway. Candles burned everywhere, and flowers graced my entire breezeway. I knew Damien was there. I walked up a few more stairs and into my house to find candles and flowers everywhere! My favorite music was playing downstairs in my art studio. I went down there.

Damien always teased me about the cheap paint-covered boom box in my studio. But now, I discovered he'd had an awesome new sound system installed. As it played, I was thrilled at his thoughtfulness. I looked around for him again, but he was nowhere to be found. Rosie, my sweet pooch, came down to see me. Her collar was all flowers! I greeted my girl and went upstairs.

My entire home was full of candles and flowers with more of the same music playing. My dining room table was set with new, gorgeous and artistic dishes. There were new, artsy placemats and cloth napkins. And there stood Damien, leaning against my kitchen counter with a bottle of our favorite wine and two new beautifully hand-painted glasses waiting for me. I cried. It was all so thoughtful and sweet. This was Damien—over-the-top romantic and sweet.

We walked into the dining room, and I was admiring the beautiful new dishes when he handed me a card that held tickets to Toronto for the weekend. My face must have reflected the apprehension and pressure I felt. Damien didn't say anything and quickly walked out to my kitchen and came back with dinner. He was not a cook, but he had a fabulous carryout dinner and served it on new dishes and platters. He insisted I just sit and relax. He was his sweet, kind, caring self.

After dinner, Damien insisted on picking up all the dishes. He said, "Give your girl some love," and Rosie looked at me. I got down on the floor with my cute little English bulldog in her flowered collar. I was admiring it, and I asked how he had ever found a collar like it. He told me his florist had made it to match all the real flowers that filled my home. He asked me to look closely at it. Under Rosie's wrinkly bulldog chin where a tag would lie was a box covered in little flowers that I had not seen. I gulped and opened it. A huge diamond gleamed. Damien said, "I'm not getting any younger. I love you. Let's take this kite and run with it. I want to spend the rest of my life caring for you. I love you. Will you marry me?"

As romantic as it was, it was a pressure that I wasn't prepared for and didn't want. I didn't know how to say no. I thought of all the kind and nice things he'd just done and what a sweet man he was, but I was not sure and Julian was in the front of my mind. I didn't want any changes before Julian graduated from high school.

I felt pressured and told him I wasn't ready as nicely as I could. I wasn't prepared for his response. He cried. He told me both of our families had played a part in making this a special engagement and they were waiting for our call. I felt terrible. Then I quickly agreed to an engagement, but explained that I would not marry him until after Julian graduated from high school. He told me to take all the time I needed, that he would always be there waiting on my yes. He told me that when I was ready, I would make him the happiest man on the planet. He said he would always make sure I was loved and cared for, married or not. The pressure was on.

Gee called me later that same night. She said she had "seen it" and that I would be very happy with him. Gee told me I would spend the rest of my life with him and to trust him, that he would care for me. Gee was always accurate. Six joy-filled months later, we would be married.

Before our wedding day, Damien brought me a prenuptial agreement. He insisted that I take it to my attorney to review. The agreement was extremely unique and completely one sided. The prenuptial said that in the case of divorce, any and all assets would go to me and any and all debt would go to Damien. He insisted before we were married to have this paperwork in place to "protect Julian." My attorney said he had never seen anything so one sided. He said, "Obviously this man loves you and believes you will be married forever." Any jitters I had seemed to be calmed by the most unlikely of places: legal paperwork.

Our wedding was intimate. Damien found a cool little chapel. Painted angels appeared all over the walls, and Damien had arranged to have one of my angel sculptures on display inside. His family filled that small artsy place. We played our favorite music and wrote our own vows. I was grateful for the new family that surrounded and welcomed us with so much love. On our honeymoon, Damien began talking to me about selling my business for the first time. He told me he didn't like having me away from him so much and that it was high time I was taken care of.

Damien was the first person in my life who I felt really loved me. I felt like he loved my heart. He was always bragging about me. He told anyone who would listen that I was the best thing that had ever happened to him. Every day, he told me I was beautiful. I have always felt far, far less than beautiful, but he began to make me feel beautiful. I had fallen deeply in love with Damien, the blond guy with the horrible laugh.

Damien was romantic and spontaneous. He would plan surprise trips and involve my staff and my father to make sure everything was handled. I'd come home from the salon to bags packed and there he'd be, tickets in hand. Damien continued to always surprise me with little things. There were gifts from my favorite boutiques, jewelry and boxes of chocolates for not only me but for Julian and my staff. He even hand delivered roses and chocolates to my entire staff on Valentine's Day. One time he sneaked Julian out of school and took him to buy a new suit and have it custom tailored for his homecoming. Those two went out to lunch and then Damien took Julian back to school. They did all of this together and told me all about it that night at dinner. It blessed me to see Damien take such good care of my baby.

Holidays were so special with his family. Lots of love, prayers, and songs went around a huge dining table. Dad and Julian were treated as if they had always been part of his huge family. It was a dream come true for me. I felt Julian could see what a real family looked like with them. My heart ached for my boy. Julian had been through so much.

64

The divorce of Justo and me, the loss of Justine, and the death of his beloved Gramma. Life had been very hard for Julian.

Damien even helped repair a fractured relationship between Justo and me. He noticed that Justo's responsibility to pay child support triggered anger from him. Damien orchestrated a reduced lump sum payment in lieu of years of future child support. He said that it would free Justo, repair the relationship between the two us, and that we did not need Justo's money. Damien assured me he would always care for any of Julian's and my needs. So I signed off on all future child support, and I thanked God for Damien. He was the family I had yearned for all my life.

The Wolf Begins to Emerge

Soon after we were married, Damien began pressuring me to sell my business. He said I needed to relax and let him love me and that it hurt him to have me spending so many hours away. Damien said, "I need to care for you."

I designed a small collection of bleach-proof clothes for my staff to wear and had them made. Soon our customers were asking where they could buy them. Yet another business was being birthed. With Damien's push, I took my designs to San Francisco, home of the largest hair color show in the country. At the show, I debuted my collection and the biggest names in the industry not only loved it, they bought the entire collection for their staffs. I was extremely excited and so was Damien. Soon I was even busier than ever, designing away, working on photoshoots, preparing models, creating websites, catalogs, packaging, and more. We were off and running together in a new and fun business that had us together twenty-four/seven. As the business grew, it became too much to run the salon. I had already turned over my entire personal clientele to my staff. Selling the salon to focus on my clothing business seemed to be the natural and right thing to do, so I sold it.

Closing day arrived, and the new owner was prepared to take over my beloved salon, spa, and gift art gallery. I had sold businesses and homes before and it was somewhat routine, but this time I felt nostalgic. The closing took place in Damien's attorney's office. For the first time, Damien seemed nervous. He called me by his ex-wife's name. I had a funny feeling in my stomach. His nervousness made me uncomfortable, unsure of the sale and suspicious. It had shocked me when he called me "Mary." Nothing like this had ever happened before, and I noticed a bizarre exchange of looks and unspoken words between Damien and his attorney.

When Damien left the room, his lawyer apologized for him and said how much Damien loved me and wanted everything to be perfect for me, including the sale of my business. I felt ashamed of my suspicions. Still, a voice inside of me was telling me not to sell my salon. I thought it was my fear of change, and I dismissed it. But I couldn't understand why Damien was so nervous. The closing paperwork was signed and a huge chunk of my hard-earned money was on the table. It was a culmination of many years of very hard work.

Damien had had his attorney prepare paperwork in advance. It looked like the prenuptial he had insisted I sign before we were married. I thought about the one-sided protection my lawyer had assured me I had with the prenuptial. With that good memory, I signed the paperwork to sell my business. At the very same time, Damien's attorney began to explain how they had set up accounts for Julians future. He had also set up investments specifically for Julian and me. I trusted him and dismissed my anxious feelings, gulped, and signed the rest of the papers. I went on with life. It was business as usual with our new and thriving clothing company.

My days were peaceful but busy. I was creating art and designing clothing, jewelry, and accessories. Damien handled books, negotiations, and component sourcing. I was excited about life and the successes Damien and I were having in our new business. I loved that we were together all the time. Slowly, over time, beginning with my salon business, I had given Damien access to my accounts and my business as he requested. Layer by layer, he soon was handling all of our finances. He had found accounting errors and suggested I use his accountant to fine tune the salon a few months before it sold. Damien and his accountant had been cleaning up errors in accounting and saving the salon money. I did not even give it a second thought when Damien assumed the business lead and I assumed the creative lead and the face for our rapidly growing clothing business. I fully and completely trusted Damien with everything in my life. I relaxed and genuinely had fun with business, his family, and life for the first time ever. Never in a million years would it have occurred to me that Damien would intentionally harm Julian or me in any way.

Damien's jovial self suddenly changed. When I would try to comfort him and ask what was wrong, he would tell me not to worry. But I was worried about him nonetheless. He was not himself. I asked about business, and he would pull up the perfect paperwork to answer my question in detail. Damien was an analytical type and extremely smart. It was a comfort and a luxury to not worry about anything and do what I do best: create.

Damien started spending more time glued to his computer. One day, he told me that our clients had begun defaulting and were not paying for merchandise that had already been shipped. Our business appeared to be a house of crumbling cards. Then one day, he very matter-of-factly said we needed to close the business. I will never forget the pit I felt in my stomach when he told me we were unable to pay our vendors and he felt declaring business bankruptcy was the only option. I was deeply saddened. Then came the first glimpse into truth.

Damien assured me this was the smartest business decision we could make. He told me about all sorts of big businesses that "reorganized" on a regular basis. He assured me it was not shameful and we would be far better off for it. He was handling the bankruptcy, and I was notifying clients of our decision to close and the liquidation sale of inventory. The stock market and the housing market had just crashed. Damien told me our customers could not pay us because they were in bankruptcy too. He asked me to come with him to his lawyer's office to sign paperwork.

When we arrived, I saw only my name and my corporation's name on every single piece of paper in front of me. His name was nowhere to be found. Immediately, I started questioning him, and in response, he looked at me with complete shock and hurt, like I had slapped him. His eyes filled with tears, and he asked how in the world I could ask him such questions. Tears rolled down his cheeks as his lawyer stood there watching us.

That was the second time I had seen tears. The first was when I said "not yet" to his proposal. Damien said that if I did not have basic trust with money, business, and finances with him, then our relationship was a fraud. He said all women had always been after his money, and he thought I was different. He managed to make me feel horrible and apologize for the scenario that I'd almost uncovered. Not until later did I learn he had used me and my salon's name and my many years of successful business to secure all sorts of debt unknown to me, beginning months before we were even married. I learned that even the lease for our clothing production house looked, on paper, like another one of my salons.

Damien had insisted on buying a new house for me. We sold my home, and Damien secured the proceeds in Julian's name. Our new home was a huge house with a sprawling lawn and a large pool. It was gorgeous and had flower gardens that I loved. There were plumbing issues that had been hidden from us and drywalled over in the new home that had begun showing black mold, which was coming from the ceiling of the garage. He had gotten lawyers involved, and we had walked away from the home. This all happened at the same time our

70

business was closing.

Gee called and told me to trust him. She said my suspicions stemmed from never having experienced real love. I believed her. Damien's oldest son, William, his wife, Anne, and their kids came to our home for dinner. Damien ran to the store for diapers they had forgotten. While he was out, William started asking me what I thought were peculiar questions. He asked me if I knew about his father's American Express account. I smiled and told him how cool I thought it was. He had a puzzled look and asked me why.

I told him that his father used that American Express for everything and that I had seen one of the statements and noticed that it had his (William's) name on it alongside his father's. I told William I had asked his father about that. Damien had told me that to establish credit for William, he had opened that card in both of their names in 1990. I told William how proud his dad was of him with his PhD and all of his accomplishments, and how his dad had said that for sentimental reasons he would always use only that card. William was agitated and seemed almost angry at me. He left for one of the bedrooms, and I could hear him shouting at Anne. Then they left abruptly. Anne called and apologized before Damien returned from the store. She said they'd been quarreling before they arrived and assured me that all was well. I dismissed any suspicion I had. Not until months later would I learn that Damien had no credit. This was a card in his son's name. William had allowed his dad to use it since 1990, many years before I met him.

Gee and the Purple File

Damien and I settled into a condo downtown and went about life. One day, Gee began calling with an unsettling message, a warning. She told me she sensed an accident and to be very careful. I began to wonder if Damien was right about my car . . .

My car was part of a nationwide recall. The news detailed crazy accounts about cars like mine speeding out of control and being unable to stop when the accelerator stuck in high speed. In the wake of these reports, I began driving a small car on loan from the dealership. Damien was insisting they give me a new car. Damien said he wasn't going to stand for a replaced part of such significance on our car and worry about my safety. He would rather trade it in then have it repaired.

Gee's calls made me nervous about a repaired accelerator too, and I was happy to have Damien's over-the-top protectiveness. I was extremely cautious driving that little loaner. Gee's calls had made me a little fearful. They escalated in frequency, and she began telling me I was in danger. Over a span of a few weeks, Gee made six or seven calls like this with the same message. It was disconcerting, and I wasn't sure what to do with her information other than to drive very carefully.

Then one day her warning became specific. Gee called to tell me I needed to find the purple file and to not tell Damien about this call. She continued to warn me. She told me I was in danger—extreme danger. Gee had always been right. I wandered into our office and there sat a purple file on top of Damien's desk. I picked it up and found an open envelope inside. It was addressed to me but had a post office box as an address. I had never had a post office box and knew nothing of Damien having one either.

As I opened the envelope, thick with paperwork folded inside, I was confused. I found certified paperwork addressed to me. I scanned it very quickly, and my heart raced faster and faster. The paperwork stated that my car had been repossessed due to nonpayment and had been sold at public auction. Had Damien lied to me? As my heart raced, I went on to read papers saying that a $9,000 lien plus all legal and court costs had been filed against me for the difference in what was owed on the car and what it was sold for. The last page was a copy of a warrant for my arrest because I hadn't shown up for any court dates! My eyes blurred with tears as I skimmed over all this again. I could barely process what I was reading. My mind and heart were in total shock. There I stood, heart pounding, my mind flooding with feelings of intense betrayal, when Damien walked in the office door.

He looked at me standing there holding the paperwork. He looked closely at the papers in my hand, and suddenly the loving eyes I knew changed. The kind face, the warm eyes that I had fallen so deeply in love with became dark, void and very, very angry. What I saw was not my husband. There was a dark and evil stare looking straight through me. Damien instantly dropped the mail and keys he held in his hands on the floor and strode quickly across the room toward me. I stepped backward, and for the first time in my life felt like I was going to be attacked. For those split seconds, I wondered if I was dreaming. When he got to me, his strong hands wrapped around my upper arms and he violently shook me. I was in disbelief. I told him he was hurting me and to stop.

Damien told me to shut up. His breath smelled like alcohol. He squeezed harder and shoved me backward. I heard myself scream as he shoved me into our bedroom. He started tearing at my clothes and literally threw me on the bed. Damien was a strong man, but at that moment he seemed extremely strong and my anger ceased as I began to fill with fear. He was shouting at me and telling me that I would "never, ever leave him." He told me, "You belong to me. You are mine."

Suddenly, it was as if he was imagining me with another man and grew viciously angry and jealous. He told me that I was lucky to have him and most women would give anything to have him. He told me women wished they had a husband like him, and he was going to remind me why. My husband raped me. When I fought back, he

74

became more violent. So I lay there and tried not to move. I stared through tears into his eyes. I thought he would stop. It made him angrier and more forceful. He told me I would never, ever leave him. The person he had just become was a complete stranger to me. I felt like I was in a nightmare and couldn't wake up. I remember noticing that I didn't cry outloud. I laid there in complete shock. My heart seemed to stop. My body was in terrible pain, and my world was in shambles.

Then as sudden as his attack was, he stood up, put his clothes on, and stormed out without saying a word. I had never in my life been hit or shoved around or hurt like this before. I didn't know what to do. I just sat with my thoughts and wondered if this had really happened. I thought about calling the police and imagined their laughter if I said that my husband had lied about money and raped me. Darkness told me the police would never believe me. I walked into the bathroom and showered with the door open. I felt dirty, ashamed, and afraid. I didn't know what to do. I now know that I was in a physical and emotional state of shock.

Suddenly, I thought about the doors and walked out in a towel quickly to deadbolt every door and window in our condo. I noticed that Damien had taken the purple file with him. Everything seemed dreamlike, unreal. My life was suddenly playing out in hyperfast motion. I hurt badly, and I desperately wanted to call Mom. I really needed her now, but she was gone. It was as if the grief of the loss of

Mom flooded back into raw newness. Like a little girl, I lay in a fetal position on the floor and cried for my mom. I could not imagine how I could ever tell Dad. Dad lived in Minnesota now and was hours away. I called Gee, but she didn't answer. I had a panicked need to call someone. I wanted to be rescued. I was so afraid Damien would come back, and I knew he had taken the only car. I didn't know whom to turn to. I thought again about calling the police. I just couldn't imagine trying to explain to anyone in my life or to the police the deception I had only started to uncover or the fact that my husband had just raped me.

That same morning when I left home had been like every other morning. We were deeply in love. We'd had coffee together and discussed life. I was reading the Bible for the first time in my life and had started with Genesis. Damien told me that it was better to start with the New Testament and so I had. We would discuss what I had read most mornings. I believe I was in the book of Mark. The person that had just done this to me was a different person, a monster I'd never met.

Gee's phone calls and warnings were racing through my mind. Then I began questioning what I had read in that purple file. Did he really have a post office box and hide mail from me? Was my car really repossessed when I thought he had taken it to the dealer? I wondered how all of this had been hidden so skillfully. It seemed like it just couldn't be possible.

Hours had gone by in the blink of an eye. It was late, and Damien still had not returned home. My mind told me Damien had left me. I thought he would never be back. A panicky feeling set in again, and I tried to reach Gee. This time she answered. She wasn't remotely surprised as I cried out details to her. Gee told me she had "seen" that I was still in extreme danger and that I needed to get out of that condo immediately. I had no car; Damien had taken it. It hurt to even walk, and I didn't know what to do. Intense fear was settling in as she warned me to run. She told me to call a friend or the police and get out of there immediately. A feeling of shame blanketed me. I imagined Julian, Dad, Damien's family, and everyone I loved hearing of the deception, my stupidity, and the physical and sexual abuse.

After a few hours of talking with Gee, I calmed down and promised her I would call 911 if Damien returned. I told her I needed to sleep on it before I called anyone. By this point, I knew Damien wouldn't be back. The condo was secured, and the neighbor was home upstairs. He would hear me scream if Damien returned. I soaked in a hot bath to relieve my aching body hoping I'd he able to sleep.

Suddenly, Damien was beating on the door very loudly and shouting my name. My heart began racing again as I realized I had been dead wrong about his reappearance. I jumped out of the tub and frantically dressed myself. Damien began calling my phone over and over when I didn't answer or let him in. I picked up my phone and was thinking that surely Jonas, the man upstairs, would be out in the hallway in light of all the noise Damien was making. Meanwhile, I couldn't make myself dial 911. It was as if darkness began blanketing me in heavy immobilizing fear.

Damien called again, and this time I answered. His beating on the door had escalated, and he was screaming my name over and over. When I answered the phone I didn't say a word, and Damien cried for the third time. He told me he loved me. He told me he was under an extreme amount of pressure and begged me to forgive him. He told me he would never begin to forgive himself for how he had hurt me, and he begged me to give him a chance. He told me he would spend the rest of his life making it up to me. He kept crying that he loved me.

Our condo was one of two in a huge, historic mansion. The grand front entrance was a tightly secured lobby with an equally grand staircase leading to a second condo, which occupied the entire second floor. Our condo was the entire first floor. The back entrance also had a large lobby that, with another staircase, led upstairs and had a door that led to our kitchen. Damien was in the back lobby with his shouts echoing loudly. They were dissolving into begging and remorse. I have no idea why I had such a foolish lapse of judgment. My mind racing, I thought of Jonas, the neighbor, and felt embarrassed by the scene that was playing out.

Shame and shock told me to let Damien in and that he would not hurt me any further. I took that bait of shame, and I let him in. Very quickly, I saw that Damien was under the influence of a whole lot of alcohol and looked completely out of his mind. He looked like a crazy man on drugs. His eyes were black and void. They were not the blue eyes I knew and loved. I was not seeing my husband but looking into the eyes of Satan, and I knew it.

He immediately resumed his extreme violence against me. He pushed, shoved, and backed me into our bedroom again and onto the bed. It was a very large king-size bed, and I scrambled to the other side. Damien was a diabetic and used insulin multiple times a day. He took his insulin out of his pocket and exposed the needle. He clicked it to inject himself, and insulin dripped out. I noticed he hadn't checked his blood sugar like he always did. The now unforgettable smell of insulin filled the bedroom. Damien didn't inject himself but started pacing around the bedroom with his insulin needle like an animal with a wild look in his eyes. He said he wondered how much insulin it would take to kill me and then laughed that horrible laugh. He said no one would ever know or see a tiny needle hole. He told me he had been reading about it on the Internet and had learned how completely untraceable insulin could be.

Damien took pleasure in seeing the intense state of fear he had put me in. He was smiling and laughing. He went to the kitchen for more beer, and I stayed frozen in fear. I thought that if I tried to leave he would catch me and surely kill me with that needle full of insulin. I thought about screaming for Jonas upstairs but thought I had heard doors shut earlier and darkness told me he was gone. Darkness told me that if I screamed or tried to run, Damian would kill me.

Damien came back with a six pack of Heineken, his favorite pleasure. He began mumbling and calling me by his pet nicknames. I was sitting with my arms wrapped around my knees in the far corner of the bed. He lay down and reached his arm toward me. Damien told me to lie beside him. I did. Eventually he passed out next to me in that bed. I lay there frozen, afraid to move. I was afraid that if he woke up, he would kill me. That was Friday night, and I would stay awake all night. I didn't leave the bed and hardly moved. I was afraid if I did, he would wake up. I prayed that when he did wake up, he would be sober and maybe a part of "him" would return.

A memory suddenly flooded my mind. Before Julian had started college and was still at home, he and I had squabbled about something insignificant, like curfew. He had smarted off a bit in a very typical teenage fashion. Damien had jumped on him harshly. That had shocked me and made me angry. But what shocked me more was what he said after Julian left. Damien said, "I wanted to blow his knees out. One kick, and he would be down." That shocked and angered me. Damien had then backed down immediately, apologizing to me. It made me angrier when he said he felt Julian needed to be out on his own and that he would pay for an apartment for him. From there, one of the very few disagreements I ever had with Damien ensued. He became extremely remorseful and apologetic. As I lay awake that night, I wondered why I didn't see him for what he was capable of and leave then.

Damien awoke very early on Saturday morning. He told me I looked terrible and to take a shower while he fixed me breakfast. I began looking everywhere for my phone as discreetly as I could, then I looked at him. He held my phone up and smiled at me before dropping it into his bathrobe pocket. I went into the bathroom and heard him talking. It sounded like he was talking to my father. I was in the bathroom with the shower running but still dressed and listening closely through the door.

I thought about how I could interrupt and talk to Dad. But he was hundreds of miles away from me. I showered and stayed in the bathroom for a long time. Almost two hours went by before Damien tried to open the door and asked me what I was doing. I came out. I sat at the table, and he put eggs and toast in front of me. When I didn't eat right away, he grew angry. I thanked him and ate. Damien drank all day Saturday and told me he was working on important things that he wanted to discuss with me later. He acted as if nothing had happened. I told him I wanted to go to the store. Somehow I thought he would fall for that, and I would run. He laughed at me and told me I wasn't going anywhere.

I spent the day in the bedroom, held captive in my own home. I prayed myself to sleep, asking God to help me. I'm not sure how much time had passed when Damien stormed in and woke me instantly into terror again. He told me that he was not going to allow me to leave him. He told me that marriage was for life and that it was a biblical law. He started talking about sin and death and God. Damien was delusional and made no sense at all. He was rambling and, I believe, under the influence of more than beer.

Later that night, Damien ordered pizza. The delivery boy came to the front lobby entrance. When I heard the buzzer and the door open as Damien stepped out into the lobby, I pictured myself racing out to the delivery boy and both of us being killed by Damien. Fear paralyzed me.

On Sunday, Damien passed out in a drunken stupor again. I found my keys, grabbed my phone from his nightstand, and ran as fast as I could to the car. I sped away. I was finally away, but I didn't know where to go or what to do. Instinctively, I kept looking into the rearview mirror. Even though I had the only car, I was still afraid that Damien was chasing me. Our condo was very close to Lake Michigan in downtown Milwaukee. I drove down to one of the parks on the lake, backed my car into a parking space, and kept it running. I feared that Damien would show up and I would have to speed out of there quickly.

I decided to call Lind, my good friend and sister-in-law, who I was very close to. Lind was calm, wise, and a strong believer in God. I looked up to her for spiritual advice and had a deep respect for her and her husband, Rob. I hoped that she would know what I should do. I began to tell her just a little about what had happened by describing the car and the paperwork and the lies I had uncovered about her brother. Lind did not seem surprised and didn't say much. I shared with her a little more detail of how he had become violent with me and the alcohol and suspected drugs, and she still didn't seem at all surprised. Then I told her Damien had threatened to kill me. That news didn't even move her. Calmly and without emotion, she said "they all," meaning Damien's family, felt he needed another intervention.

Lind went on to tell me stories about Damien's addiction to alcohol and how it had almost destroyed their family over many years. I descended into deeper shock and was not even really processing what she was saying. I could hardly believe that she was not surprised to learn he had been violent. I felt physically sick as Lind began telling me that she would not "take sides."

I hung up in an even deeper place of complete shock and called Dad, who was 350 miles away. I did not tell him any details but asked if I could stay with him for a while and if he would come and get me because I didn't have a car. I had no idea who actually owned the car I was driving. I explained to my father that I needed a place to stay for a little while because Damien had an escalating drinking problem. Strangely enough, Dad asked very few questions and agreed to get me. It had been many years since I had left home, and now there I was asking my father to come and get his adult daughter. I cleaned myself up to the best of my ability in the car, and I called Julian. Complete shame engulfed me as I dialed my phone. How could I ever explain to him what had happened?

I don't really remember what I told him, only that I tried to be calm and to assure him that everything was okay. I told Julian that Damien had a drinking problem. He wasn't surprised and acted like he was glad that I was leaving Damien. I wondered if I had imagined that.

Later, Dad came and, as hard it is to believe, we went back to that condo. With my father by my side, I walked into my home and grabbed my dog, Rosie, and a grocery bag full of clothes, makeup, and a toothbrush. Damien wasn't there, but he called me when we were in the house. He told me he had walked to a drug treatment facility nearby and had asked for help. Damien said he had "started a program and to please not leave him." I didn't respond. Within minutes, he was standing in the house and in front of Dad and me, crying and begging for forgiveness. I quickly grabbed my things without saying much, and Dad and I left. Dad realized things were far more serious than I'd let on, but he said very little. We were on the freeway and not yet out of the city when I received the first of three bizarre phone calls.

My phone rang within fifteen minutes. My bank was calling to let me know that my cards had just been canceled because there'd been a fraud reported on the account. They said new cards would be mailed to me the following week. I asked them what had happened, and they said Damien had called to report fraudulent charges and asked to have new cards issued and the existing ones canceled immediately. I gave them Dad's address so that they would send the new cards to me. They said I would have to come into my local bank to authorize the cards to be sent to any address besides my Wisconsin one. It was Sunday night and the twenty-four-hour fraud hotline told me to go into the local bank the next morning. We continued driving to Minnesota. I later learned that the twenty dollar bill in my purse was all that I had left to my name.

The second call came from Dorothy, my mother-in-law. She was crying and said, "Please don't leave me. I cannot bear to lose another one. I love you, Ada. Please don't leave. Please forgive me!" I tried to explain without embarrassing details what had happened. Dorothy didn't seem surprised either. Dad listened closely as he drove. I wondered what "another one" meant or why she was asking for my forgiveness. It had been almost forty-eight hours since I'd slept, and I was almost incoherent by this point. My body hurt, my heart was broken, and my mind was confused and turning in circles. Nothing was making sense. After Dorothy hung up, I fell asleep in the car as Dad drove us silently to his home in Minneapolis.

I was awakened by the sound of my phone ringing about an hour later. This time it was Damien's youngest child, Joshua. He was a sweet boy whom I'd grown very close to. Josh was in college. He had spent many nights at our home for dinner and games around the table with his girlfriend. I loved Joshua very much. When I answered the phone, he immediately told me he loved me and that he didn't blame me. Just like Dorothy, it was as if he knew something I didn't. Everything was so very surreal.

I slept the rest of the way to Minneapolis. I don't remember getting there or even going to bed that night. It was as if I had left Milwaukee and woke up the next morning in Dad's guest bedroom in Minnesota. When I woke up, I looked around the room and thought about how I'd arrived there. There I was, sleeping on a small antique twin bed that my mother had called the "princess bed." My art adorned the walls of my father's guest bedroom. Mom seemed to permeate everything in my father's home even though she had never lived there. My heart yearned for her. The grief of losing Mom was new again and raw. I stood there disoriented and feeling that I needed Mom to survive. Shockwaves coursed through me when I began to walk around the room. My body ached, but it was my heart that was broken. I looked in a mirror that hung above an antique dresser, and I did not recognize myself. I was swollen, battered, and very, very afraid.

I showered, found a change of clothes in the brown paper bag, and tried to gather my thoughts over a cup of coffee with Dad. Today, my precious daddy and I are extremely close. I love Dad with all of my heart. This was the first time we were together alone without Mom. It felt awkward and unfamiliar without her. He asked me how long I would be staying. My heart sank into my stomach. Fear of the unknown coursed through me.

I decided to call Damien's son William. I loved him dearly and always felt I was loved by him. Anne answered his phone. She was not herself. For the first time ever, our conversation was uncomfortable. In a monotone voice, Anne told me that she knew everything and then she became very quiet. I told her Damien had threatened to kill me, and she said she knew. I broke into tears, and she hung up. William and Anne would never see or speak to me ever again. I never saw or spoke to any of Damien's family except his precious daughter ‚Jane, ever again. His four sisters, their husbands, and all the kids and grandkids, all the people that had become my family never spoke to me again. As quickly as they all came into my life, they suddenly disappeared.

Jane and I were extraordinarily close. Our relationship had blossomed with the birth of her only child and beautiful daughter, Anna. I had taken care of Anna every Friday since she was only a few weeks old. My phone rang, and I broke into tears when I heard Jane's voice. I didn't know what to say. She said, "I tried to warn you many times.

You just did not seem to hear. You guys seemed so happy. We all thought Dad had changed. We thought you were different. We really thought you guys were in love and that he had changed." She went on to say, "Ever since he got out of prison, he was always after a quick, easy million bucks." She said, "Money owns my dad and rules his life. And he is a serious alcoholic." I felt myself collapse inside. I fell into a state of physical and emotional shock as I heard her speak. My heart raced, and my eyes blurred with tears. When I tried to ask her more questions, Jane said she and Anna loved me and then she hung up.

In desperation, I went to a local shelter close by for abused women. I told them only a small portion of what had happened and asked for advice. They filed police reports right away and then took me immediately in to see a counselor. As I walked through the shelter to her office, I noticed many women and kids in different rooms interacting with each other. They all looked up at me as I walked by and smiled a knowing smile. We felt a connection on a deep and instinctive level with one another.

I had sat with the counselor, Dr. Barnes, several times over the course of a week when she leaned over to me and took my hands in hers. Dr. Barnes told me I was suffering from post-traumatic stress disorder (PTSD) and needed to take a prescribed drug. She also recommended that I remove myself from Dad's house immediately and begin regular one-on-one counseling and support groups at the shelter. Dr. Barnes recommended that I apply for a restraining order right away and said the shelter would help me.

Dr. Barnes's words echoed in my ears. I thought that anyone would be in shock after going through what I had, and drugs were not going to change anything. I also wondered how a piece of paper, a restraining order, could protect me from anything. Dr. Barnes's words intensified the fear that was already growing inside of me. Dr. Barnes, the shelter, and the police all told me that I was in extreme danger. So did Gee, every single day. But I couldn't fully process what had happened or how truly serious it was. It was like the shock had numbed me to the severity of it. Sometimes I felt like I was in a dream, a nightmare, and that I'd wake up.

People asked me questions, and I wanted to answer but I couldn't find the words to speak. The doctor told me that this was symptomatic of PTSD and that the drugs would help me. I'm not really sure why, but I refused the drugs. I felt like I was slowly dying inside. Gee called me multiple times a day, and many days I felt like she was my only lifeline. The people at the shelter were kind and helpful, but I couldn't comprehend that I needed to be there. I didn't know what to do or how I would start over again. I was profoundly alone. I wondered if God was hearing my prayers and if He loved me.

Damien called me multiple times every day. He would leave long, pleading, and apologizing messages. Emails poured in by the dozen. Some of them begged for forgiveness, others were threatening or crude and sexual. Sometimes he would threaten me, and then another email would come begging me to meet him for a romantic weekend getaway. Damien's complete delusion terrified me and so did the thought of the complete deception I'd been living in so blindly.

I thought about the things Jane had told me about her father, like the fact he had been in prison. I thought about what Damien had told me when I first met him. When we first started dating, Damien had told me about a business partner he had many years before and how that partner had lied and tried to steal money from him. He said they had been involved in some sort of business deal and his partner had become extremely greedy and deceptive. Damien said this man lied to others about him and because of it, he had lost a lot of money on a business deal and so had the partner. He said this guy had him arrested in 1990 and tried to blame him for things that did not happen. When Damien told me this, he was embarrassed because of the arrest on his record and explained that he basically was told he had paid himself too much from his own company.

It was the first birthday of Mom's after her death, and Julian was with his father. Damien and I had not been dating long. He lifted my spirits that day with a surprise day trip to Chicago. It was a wonderful surprise and a really fun day. When we returned to Milwaukee, I met his mother and sisters for the first time. The day had been enchanted and joyful, Damien told me casually as he dropped me off at my house that night. We had continued to sit in his car in front of my home. He opened up the conversation about being arrested, I asked questions, and he told me mostly about how he'd been surprised by his partner's lack of character. He appeared embarrassed and seemed to be totally transparent. He asked if I had any other questions, and I told him no. The next morning I shared with my father what Damien had told me and asked for his opinion. Dad said it took guts to tell me the truth and it had been many, many years ago. He said he respected Damien for his honesty and that we all had experienced things we would rather not have been through.

Now when I began researching Damien to uncover exactly what Jane had started to tell me, it looked entirely different than what I had always believed to be true. I learned more about Damien and who he really was, and that I was not alone, there were others like me. Arrest and court records began to tell the story. The court records revealed shocking details. What I saw was multiple counts of racketeering, embezzlement, fraud, and theft. He had been given a ten-year prison sentence. I contacted state's attorneys, police departments, and public records and began to dig very deeply into the truth. What I was now beginning to uncover looked nothing like what I was told that day. Damien was a convicted felon and a thief.

Learning all of these facts and knowing the truth lessened my fear and gave me a little self-confidence. There is a power in knowing the truth, and this truth was giving me the strength I needed to move forward. I responded to a few of Damien's emails and thought that I truly was in control. I started to communicate with him a little by little over the phone and email. I thought I was in the driver's seat and manipulating him as I dug for more information.

I wanted to retrieve my personal belongs and keepsakes from the condo. As Damien begged for a romantic weekend getaway, I told him I needed time first and that I hoped we could work through things. Damien agreed when I told him I wanted to pick up my things from our condo. Through emails, he agreed to not come near our home for three days while Dad and I were there. Still, Damien begged me to just "come home" and "let him love me." He said he would do anything to show me his love. I felt confident that I was in control and that he would do anything to make me stay with him. I reiterated that I needed time to think and that it was my hope that we would reconcile and start over in Minnesota. Of course, I had no intention of ever seeing him again. Damien seemed happy, and he promised me that he wouldn't be there.

Gee kept calling and telling me over and over that I was in danger. When I insisted on going back for my belongings, Gee asked if I remembered her "hearing" that I would spend the rest of my life with him. She said, "Don't cut your life short. Don't go." That scared me, but foolishly I really felt that I would be safe with Dad with me. Two of his friends were going to drive up a day behind us with a big truck and help. I felt Gee was overreacting. The crying and remorse that I had heard coming from Damien had assured me that he would never try to harm me again. In hindsight it seems ridiculous, but at the time the shock and disbelief had truly convinced me that I was in control and would be safe. I still remembered the man I loved and who loved me so much. I wondered if financial stress has caused him to snap. I thought he would never do anything to harm me, and after all, Dad would be with me . . .

il-lu-sion:

A thing that is or is likely to be wrongly perceived or interpreted by their senses. A deceptive appearance or impression. A false idea or belief. Dictionary.com

Damien was standing at the stove as I unlocked the back door and let myself in. He turned slowly, smiling and wearing the suit he had worn only once, for our wedding. That image, the fear that flooded into my mind, and the instinct to run but standing there frozen will remain with me forever. I just stood there, unable to say anything. Why had I not stayed outside with my father as he walked our dogs? I stepped back as Damien came toward me, his eyes cold and evil, and he asked me for a hug.

Why had I believed him again? Before I could say anything, he said he was leaving and just wanted to say hi. I walked quickly into my office, a huge room with a large bay window overlooking the front walk where I knew Dad was. I sat down at a conference table in the middle of the window, with my back to my dad, facing the entrance I had just come in. When I heard the door shut, I was relieved. I looked and saw my dad outside talking to someone and I assumed it was Damien. Then I heard footsteps coming toward the office. I looked up. Damien was coming quickly with huge strides toward me saying, "I am going to strangle you." I stood up as he grabbed ahold of my neck. I managed to say, "Get your hands off me!" Fear paralyzed me as Damien gripped my neck. Gee's warnings flooded my mind as he shook me. I could see Dad with the dogs but couldn't make a sound. I wondered if this was how I was going to die.

Julian had come in the back door at the exact same time. He had heard me tell Damien to get his hands off me. In that split second, Julian looked at the block of knives on the counter and stopped, remembering a movie where the knife was turned around on the victim and instead he reached for a heavy metal pepper mill. When he did, he knocked the matching metal salt grinder to the floor. Damien stopped when he heard it hit the floor. I gasped as we both looked over to see Julian racing around the corner. Damien let go of me and calmly said, "Hi, buddy!"

Julian and I have been through a lot of heartache together, but violence was something we'd never experienced. Julian yelled at Damien to get away from his mom, and Damien left quickly. I felt like I had lost my mind and will never forget the look in Damien's eyes. I had seen complete demonic hatred, void of any shred of the man I thought I knew. Damien hated me and clearly wanted me dead. There was no longer any confusion or doubt about this. My entire being fragmented as questions flooded my mind. *Was our entire life together a fraud? Did he plan this? Did he ever love me? How could I not have known?* I thought we were deeply in love. I thought for the first time in my life I had gotten it right. *How did this happen to Julian and me?*

As I reflect on the next series of events, it seems almost too crazy to be real, but I assure you, it was real. Julian was extremely shook up and very angry. He wanted to go after Damien. I downplayed everything again and told him I was fine. I asked him to not overreact. I tried to convince him that Damien was just freaked out because I was moving out. I told Julian that I didn't want to upset Grampa and for him to just try and let it go. It was late afternoon, and Dad came in with our dogs. Dad said he'd talked to Damien briefly outside, but he'd been in a hurry to leave. Then Dad, Julian, and I went out for dinner! Julian and I told Dad a little of what had happened but downplayed and sugarcoated it as we drove downtown. The entire scene was surreal. We went to Dad's favorite downtown spot, Ella's. We ordered cosmos and Dad's favorite appetizers. I was shaking inside as I calmly sipped that pink drink trying to act nonchalant. Because I had withheld things, Dad didn't completely process how serious *anything* was. I tried to cover everything to protect Julian as we sat and ate dinner a few hours after my husband had tried to strangle me. It seems impossible that this was the case now, but I never even considered calling the police.

I'm not sure why I kept covering for Damien, but I believe it was shame and fear wrapped up with complete denial. We dropped Julian off at his apartment and went back to that condo to pack my things. I was in a daze, and Dad seemed jumpy and maybe just a little scared from the innuendo he had picked up on at dinner. I wondered if Julian had told him more when I had gone to the ladies' room or if he just sensed danger. The bruising did not show until the next day, but the emotional battering was evident. I collapsed into a puddle of tears as I entered what only days before had been my joyfilled home.

Damien called almost immediately. I answered and told him not to come near the building, or I would dial 911. Damien laughed and said that was ridiculous. He said he didn't want to be where he wasn't loved, appreciated, or wanted. Again, as crazy as it sounds, he made me feel responsible for his sadness. Even through all the fear, I actually felt sorry for him because he had no place to go. Today I ask myself why I didn't call 911 right away. Denial does that. Darkness does that. It whispers in your ear that somehow you deserve it and are responsible to fix it for everyones sake. Darkness told me I was shaming my family again. Darkness told me how stupid I was to not have known. Darkness told me what a failure I was.

Without saying a word, Dad and I went right to work packing. My mind continued to race in circles of how's and why's. The fear of Damien trying to come back made me frantically throw anything that mattered to me into boxes. I walked into the guest room and stood in front of Damien's huge walk-in closet. I was determined to retrieve the personal pictures I had stored there. Something prompted me to pull aside a long line of his shirts hanging above his pants. On that hidden shelf sat a large men's jewelry box wrapped with electrical tape!

I took the box out, sat down on the bed, and unwound the tape. Inside I found only one thing: a neatly folded piece of paper tucked in a tiny drawer. As I unfolded it, I recognized it as a page from a journal I had written many years before I had ever met Damien. If I'd been standing, my knees would have buckled when I unfolded the paper. In the last year of her life, Mom had encouraged me to be open to love again. One afternoon she suggested that I write down what I wanted in a husband. I'd never done anything like this before and found it to be healing. I'd written down in almost prayerlike form all of what I had ever dreamed of in a husband. Like a checklist, Damien had become every single thing I had written on that list. I laid down on the bed, literally sick to my stomach. Dad came in, and I showed him the jewelry box and what I had found inside it. It visibly scared my father. I stood at the bathroom sink and splashed my face with cold water. The bruising on my neck was beginning to show.

My father and I started searching that closet very closely. We found multiple years of tax records. None of them had Damien's correct name, but they all had his signature. On some, his first name was switched with his middle name. Some had different middle names and some had different first names. It appeared to be tax fraud. Other wives I had never heard of before were listed on the tax forms. I only knew of Mary, of the mother of his kids. All of these tax forms had his handwriting with a slightly varied signature. I shoved them into a box, took them outside, and locked them in the trunk of Dad's car. I took the journal pages and tucked them into my purse.

In that same closet we also found a life insurance policy that Damien had taken out on me several months earlier. Damien had said he'd purchased it to support his friend who was selling insurance. At the time, I thought nothing of it. Damien had told me he had overlooked the fact that I did not have any life insurance and had assumed I did. He had showed me paperwork, and I had signed it. I hadn't given it a second thought. I trusted him. As I now looked at all this with a whole new understanding, I began to crumble inside.

The man I had been so in love with, my husband, had purchased a life insurance policy and then had tried to kill me. I took the papers and continued quickly packing. My fear was just about more than I could handle. I rested on knowing that Dad's friend would be there early in the morning with his truck. In a few hours, I would be out of there. Dad and I went to bed around midnight. I was asleep in my room, and Dad insisted on sleeping on the couch instead of in the guest room. I didn't know that he was sleeping with one eye open and a packing knife in his hand.

Dad had just fallen asleep when the front door opened and awakened him. It was Damien. Damien actually sweet-talked Dad into letting him sleep in the guest bedroom. He convinced him that he was devastated to be losing his daughter and that he would do anything to "win me back." Damien was in tears and said he had nowhere to go and that he'd help load the truck the next day. Dad agreed. I knew about none of this because I had slept through it all.

Dad awakened a little later just as Damien crept into my room. I woke up to Damien grabbing me and demanding the papers from the closet. I screamed as Dad charged into the room. I told myself that this couldn't be real. It was like a movie scene. There was my aging father with a packing knife defending me from my husband. It's hard to believe, but Damien ended up sleeping in the guest room and my father walked him to the car and gave him back all the tax papers the next morning. Dad shouted at me to go to my bedroom and let him handle it, and I did. I was up all night afraid in my room, and Dad was awake and fearful on the couch. Damien slept in the guest bedroom and left very early the next morning.

Dad and I checked the garage together. I realized how I'd seldom been in the garage as Dad and I entered. What we found was shocking. There were multiple huge black garbage bags filled with empty NyQuil bottles and beer bottles—hundreds of them.

When we walked back into my home, I saw my reflection in a mirror. I had bruising and broken blood vessels in my eyes. With no sleep and all the tears, I was a complete wreck. I put makeup on to hide the pain. Dad's friend arrived with the truck and my brother Michael. As they very quickly packed up the vehicle, I stood on the curb hugging Julian and sobbing. I never imagined not being in the same town as my baby. I was crushed in spirit, in my soul, and in my body. We drove back to Minneapolis.

I thought about how Gee had said Damien was my soulmate and that I would spend the rest of my life with him. I thought about how in a way, I almost had. He almost ended my life. I thought about the life insurance policy to help a friend. I wondered if he had really planned to kill me when he bought it. I would learn that Damien was stalking me long before we met. He had targeted me. I was single, successful in business, owned my own home, and in an extremely vulnerable time when he made his move.

I thought about the one-sided prenuptial agreement and all the paperwork. It was not that he never thought we would divorce. I was coming to realize that he planned to bury me from the first time we met. That paperwork was put in place to lure me into complete trust. I was not ever going to leave that relationship alive. I pulled my dog, Rosie, up in bed with me and finally fell asleep. In my sleep, God came to me with a feeling of peace. I opened my eyes and felt His presence in the room in the form of a peace in the midst of hell. God's presence and peace allowed me to sleep. I felt His true protection was with me and wondered if it had been with me for a very long time.

I remembered reading that God will never give you more than you can handle and will always provide a way to escape. I was blessed to have walked away not once but twice from extreme violence. That night I felt God tell me that He was my protector and to trust Him. My husband and my world had just discarded me as trash. My heavenly Father comforted me and helped me sleep.

Abba

For you have not received a spirit of bondage to fear;
but you have received a spirit of adoption,
by which we cry Abba Father.
Romans 8:15

The first days at Dad's disappeared like vapor as the days blurred together. Intense nightmares stole my sleep. Over and over, Damien would catch me as I ran from him. He would squeeze my neck as he stared into my eyes. His eyes were black and dry like a piece of coal. My body was limp, unable to move or fight back. I'd awaken just before I died.

Shock and sleep deprivation left me barely able to function. My once joyful heart was fragmented in a million jagged pieces. Grief and deep spiritual pain gripped me from the inside out. Abandonment, betrayal, and confusion filled my mind. Primal fear now surrounded the man I so deeply loved. I knew God had protected me from death. I wondered why.

How could I have been so deceived? Was my world a lie from the beginning? This shock was only the beginning of what lay ahead. Sometimes God only shows us a little at a time. If I'd learned all that had taken place, and all at once, I don't think my heart could've handled it. Life came at me like water from a fire hose when tiny sips of water was really all I could handle.

I dissolved into tears. Any strength I thought I had was gone. Intense grief, shame, and fear wrapped me with desperate loneliness. Julian was hundreds of miles away for the first time in our lives. He deserved so much better than me. Shame crushed my soul.

In my desperation and loneliness, I wanted to call my sister-in-law Lind or stepdaughter, Jane. They'd become my family and closest friends. It was then, in that moment, the realization of the family betrayal and the extreme isolation I'd experienced started settling into my bones. It took my breath away. Damien's family had known everything and chosen to keep secrets.

The thought of my brothers brought deep hurt. We were a dysfunctional disaster, not a family. For many years, I'd tried to win my brothers' affections, approval, and love unsuccessfully. Any shred of decency they showed me evaporated when Mom died. It came to pass that Michael would be the only one to even speak to me and then only for a while.

I thought about the many friends and colleagues I'd worked with for years. I'd had many people in my world before I met Damien. One by one, relationships had vanished. This happened gradually after Damien entered my life, not suddenly. Damien gave me the love and protection I had always craved. My whole life, I had yearned for love, acceptance from my family, and protection. I learned that Damien had been behind the drifting friendships. One by one, he had skillfully eliminated them. He completely isolated me from my world, even my church. Damien had wanted private time as a married couple with God. This had been new and special to me. He had watched and supported a TV ministry when we met. We began watching as he prepared and served us breakfast in bed, where we prayed together. It was a natural progression and start of a new life with Damien. I never looked back. I had seen Damien as a blessing. I had trusted him and his family completely.

Dad was angry with Damien for what he had done to me. He was frustrated with my despondency and didn't know how to help. I'd disrupted Dad's world and felt shame in doing so. I spent many hours at the park down the street in the cold with a devotional book and a Bible. Every day, I'd find the Scriptures the devotions had listed for the day. Gradually, the Bible came alive to me. I was able to understand God's language, and I'd hear Him speak to me through His words in the Bible.

I was always afraid in that park and sensed that Damien was stalking me. Fear began to shackle my thoughts, taking residence deep inside of me. Fear defined who I was and how I lived. I was waiting for

Damien to show up. I prepared myself for the inevitable, and many days just wanted to get it over with. It became a silent resolve as I watched and waited, wondering when he would appear. The thought of his hands around my neck was terrifying, and I hoped he would shoot me instead.

While sitting on that park bench, I pondered many things from childhood. I thought about running away and being a disappointment to my family as a kid. I wondered if I had been born a boy if things would have been different. Maybe my brothers would have liked me? I have vivid memories of the day Tommy died and how everything changed. Dad was out of town on business and my aunt Jeanette was there. Tommy had stopped breathing while he was just sitting in his little seat on the kitchen table right beside me. I thought my heart was going to explode. Because I had played with my friend Reneé, who had been sick with German measles, I felt Tommy's death was my fault. After all, I was the reason mom had caught the illness when she was pregnant with Tommy. Because I felt I had caused Tommy's death, shame, rejection, and self-hatred had began to define me as a young girl.

I only felt peace when I focused on God. I started attending a nearby church. Dad gave me directions and the keys to his car. When I pulled into the building's parking lot, I was surprised at the size of the church. It was huge, megachurch huge. I felt very self-conscious and hoped that people wouldn't notice me in my brokenness. Love greeted me as I came in. I went into the very large sanctuary and sat on the second level and as far back as possible, close to an exit. From where I sat, I could see Damien if he walked in. The lights dimmed and music engulfed the sanctuary in a corporate praise that I'd never experienced. They were all singing with their arms raised. I suddenly felt God was present in a way I never had before. My hands raised seemingly by themselves, and I began to praise God like I never had. It felt like He was really there.

The people who were sitting and standing around me were so kind. They acted like they didn't notice what I felt was my glaring pain and physical bruising. A pastor began to speak about hopelessness, abandonment, and abuse. In the midst of thousands of people, I felt like I was the only one in the room. It was as if the pastor was speaking directly to me. He spoke of the disappointment he had been to his family. He spoke of the physical and emotional abuse he had suffered. He spoke of the suicidal pit he had found himself in the night he met God personally.

He said Abba came to him on a night he had contemplated suicide. I wondered what Abba meant just as he began to explain that it means "Daddy" in Hebrew. I could not hold back tears as he explained how deeply loving it was to use the term Abba in Scriptures. He taught me that our Abba was loving in an agape, completely unconditional, and almost nonhuman way. Total love. Abba was love, and Abba was his daddy, and Abba was my daddy too. The pastor's words were like oxygen, like CPR to a dying soul and very weary spirit. God's presence was palpable in the sanctuary. When the music started playing again, many people stood and some walked to the stage for prayer. Everyone around me left.

I could hardly stand and couldn't walk. I fell to the floor on my knees. With my head on my lap, I wept on the floor in the upper part of a gigantic sanctuary all alone. God was no longer such a mystery. I cried out to Him. I asked Him to come to me if He really was alive, if He really was real. I asked Him to show me that what the pastor had said was true. Suddenly, hands came from behind this movie-theater-style seat and lifted me back into it. I was embarrassed and felt like I had made a scene. I wiped my face a little bit and turned around to thank whoever had helped me up off the floor. No one was there! Thousands of empty seats, and no one was there! I had just met Him. He was real! That moment changed everything. I knew He was holding me. I knew Jesus had lifted me up. He was real, and He was there with me.

I cried tears of relief and joy. When I lifted my head from my hands, the pastor was in front of me and said he saw me as he was leaving. He asked if he could pray for me. He was gentle, kind, and soft-spoken, and I answered the only way I knew how. I said, "No, I am okay. I am so sorry to have kept you." Then I jumped up to leave. He grabbed me, and he just hugged me. I wept in a stranger's arms. He did not say a word. He just held me. I felt love. I felt God's Love through him. I will never, ever forget that day. Abba had come to me in a megachurch through an abused man named Tim. Tim took his abuse and turned it into an amazing ministry that had just changed the course of my life. I had an Abba. And He came to me. And He was a king! That meant I was His princess, Abba's girl. The fear seemed to melt off of me. I suddenly felt a comfort I had never, ever known.

The Knife, My Neck, and the Needle

I'm often asked if I ever had suspicions or sensed that things were not as they seemed. The answer is that if I ever had even the slightest thought cross my mind, it is as if Damien knew it before I spoke and quickly put my mind at ease. He finished my sentences and showered me with affection, love, and care. That man continued with flowers and surprise gifts the entire time we lived together. I had truly felt loved for the first time in my life. Except for one very important factor: intimacy.

This isn't an easy thing for me to share, but it is important. Our intimacy had become demanding, loveless, and what I now realize was abuse. It went from normal and loving to expectations of twice a day, every single day, no matter what. For example, after outpatient female surgery, I was in a lot of pain with intense cramping. He flat out demanded sex and was angry when I said no. He would say, "If you don't take care of your wife, someone else will. I love my wife, and I'm going to keep her the happiest woman on the planet."

I tried many times to talk to Damien, and he'd respond with hurt feelings and act as if I'd rejected him and his manhood. I am a very private person and had no one to talk to about things like this. Every time I'd try to talk to him, he convinced me that twice a day was how healthy marriages stayed vital. He'd say, "Do you honestly think that every woman in America would not want a man who is crazy about them?! Come on! I'm crazy about you, Ada! I can't get enough! I love you!" But the truth is, it felt abusive and loveless and extremely controlling. It made me question myself. I thought about how every other facet of our lives was full of love and affection, yet our intimacy was loveless. My heart was heavy with guilt for feeling that way. In every other way, he spoiled me and cared for me. Intimacy left me feeling very used and alone. I felt like something was wrong with me.

About a week before everything was exposed with that purple file, I experienced an internal alert that I didn't understand. Damien seemed to disconnect with me on an emotional level quite abruptly although the loveless and demanded intimacy stayed the same. He seemed distant and as if he was lost in thought all the time. It was as if I suddenly became invisible to him with the exception of sex. I talked to him about it. He assured me that I'd just grown accustomed to feeling rejected because of my brothers and that nothing would ever separate his love for me. But the feelings lingered. I wondered if he was having an affair. It was not a feeling of jealousy over another woman; it was a feeling of him being separated from me on a spiritual and emotional level.

One night I had an open prophetic vision for the first time in my life. I didn't understand it and felt something maybe was wrong with me. I was standing in our kitchen by the sink, emptying the dishwasher, when he grabbed a handful of silverware from the dishwasher door. Suddenly and instinctively, I jumped and screamed very loudly and quickly turned around. It scared both of us, and I felt ridiculous. I'd just experienced an extremely real vision:

I saw him with a butcher knife in his hand with a laughing, mocking look on his face. His arm drew back, and he smiled as he prepared to stab me in my back! It was an open vision that I now know was a spiritual warning from God. I didn't understand my feelings at all. It had startled both of us when I jumped and turned around screaming. I was embarrassed, and he seemed to think it was really funny. He laughed hysterically. I didn't tell him what I'd seen. He thought he'd startled me. But God was warning me.

A few days later, he almost choked me. Damien had never hurt me in any way. There was never any bondage or anything like that in our intimate life. In a moment of intimacy, he placed his hands around my neck and gripped me hard. I could not breathe. An internal voice told me to not overreact and to make eye contact. I saw that Damien was taking huge pleasure in that moment. It scared me, and I reacted with my knee in a way that pushed him away instantly. I jumped up and asked what he was doing. Damien immediately began apologizing with deep remorse at the thought of hurting me. He said he didn't realize he'd had his hands on my neck. Multiple domestic abuse experts later told me that Damien had been exhibiting textbook

112

sociopathic behavior. He fantasized about killing me. He took pleasure in looking into my eyes as he choked me.

All of this had rushed through my head when he held me captive in our bedroom. These warnings had flashed in my mind when he paced around with his insulin needle in his hand, glaring at me and telling me I wasn't leaving him. He'd told me he'd researched the effects of insulin on a nondiabetic and that I would die of shock within minutes, leaving no clue as to my cause of death. He'd told me no one would ever see a tiny needle hole in my body. My ears had heard those words, but my heart had cried out to God. I had begged God to save me. I had no idea how truly deep this betrayal and web of lies really was. A few hours later, when I'd gotten out and ran, I'd had no idea this would be the beginning of almost two years of homelessness and desperate fear.

Depression, Drugs, and the Dog

I will never leave you or forsake you.
Joshua 1:5

I spent many days at the women's shelter with a counselor or sitting numbly in a circle of women discussing their abusers. They were from all walks of life. The affluent and those on welfare sat in the same circle. I learned quickly that "DV," domestic violence, is not a respecter of wealth, education, or address. Many women had children with them. Julian was safe with friends and attending college.

My counselors pressured me to take medication for PTSD. I understood that I was numb, in shock, and not functioning normally. Taking medication would only dull my sadness, not change my circumstances. Instead, I leaned on God and nightly phone calls to Gee. The police and counselors pushed me to file for a restraining order. The thought of taking legal action against Damien terrified me. I couldn't take another fragment of fear. There was not a piece of paper in existence that would deter Damien. I thought it might make him angrier. The counselors felt I should leave Dad's house. They were right. The stress I was putting on Dad was too much. His home was a pressure cooker of emotions. I had no car and a very small amount of money saved from doing hair for people along the way.

I called my cousin Winnie, and she invited me to her home in Iowa.

Winnie has been through a lot of pain in her life. She has struggled with depression too. Dad agreed to drive me halfway to Iowa to meet Winnie and her friend. I hadn't seen her in years, but she looked like the same Winnie. She was depressed, sarcastic, and the very minute we were on the road to Iowa, out came the marijuana. Winnie and her friend smoked weed the entire way, speeding along that interstate. I sat in the backseat of that old car with my newfound addiction: coffee and cigarettes. The heaviness, the guilt, and the shame lessened as the drive continued, and I hoped my Dad felt peace. The windows were down in that old car, and it gave me a sophomoric sense of freedom as the wind whipped through that backseat and my hair. Quietly, I prayed that I would find work and a future in Iowa. Maybe I would start new in the hometown I had run away from so many years before. Somehow in that cloud of smoke, God still gave me hope.

What we walked into at Winnie's shocked me. Her apartment was in an old two-story home in "the hood." As we climbed a steep staircase to her apartment, the smell of urine and smoke accosted us. Her dog greeted us as we walked in and so did an even heavier smell of urine, pot, and cigarettes. Winnie's dog had been urinating in her carpeted apartment for what appeared to be years. I tried not to gasp. None of it seemed to affect Winnie.

It was dark, depressing, and spiritually very heavy in her home and the entire neighborhood. I was shocked and had never seen anything like the interior of Winnie's home. Little mountainlike piles of dog hair,

115

dust, and dirt stood literally inches above the picture frames that hung on the walls. The place was heavy with cigarette and pot smoke. A beat-up, urine-soaked chair faced a huge, ancient television. An eight-inch ring around the skirted bottom of the chair was sticky and amber colored from years of dog urine. The chair had duct-taped holes and dozens of burned holes from cigarettes and joints, as did the carpeted floor around it. Winnie saw me staring at it and laughed. She said, "Love me, love my dog." I told her I was worried that it appeared she had fallen asleep with burning cigarettes often. She shrugged. I sat on a dirty loveseat in the corner. What I was looking at took my breath away. I wondered if anyone else in our family had seen it.

That first night, Winnie gave me a blanket and told me to sleep on the loveseat. It was so small that halfway through the night, I opted for the floor. That's when I realized the entire carpeted floor was saturated in dog urine. My heart broke for Winnie. I loved her and wanted to help. I had a little bit of money, and we went to the store and bought all sorts of cleaners and some paint. She always had very nice things in her home, and I wondered where it all went. I learned that everything had been stored for many years in unopened boxes after a move. I found those boxes and began unpacking. Winnie was annoyed and left to see her friends. While I was cleaning, I decided to surprise her. I painted a vibrant chili pepper border on the walls around a bright red booth to match all her unearthed chili pepper decore I had found. A little TLC and an artist's touch had her home looking and smelling great in a few days. It gave me joy to do and made Winnie smile as she came home each day observing the transformation.

Winnie spent her days at her friend's house, but I could see she was happy each night when she returned and inspected what I had done that day. I colored her gray hair and gave her a cute new hairstyle. Winnie now had a smile, a pep in her step, and decided to wear makeup. She was beginning to shed the heaviness that had entrapped her. I encouraged her to believe in God and to believe in herself again. I told her about Abba and the church I'd found. The healing that was happening was in me. In helping Winnie, I found hope—hope and a purpose for living. Winnie and I spent many evenings at her friend Sue's home. Sue had breast cancer and was in the last year of her life. I talked to them about my faith, God, and heaven. They listened, and I strung beads and painted shoes. I started to see Winnie's beautiful heart emerge from her battered past.

She invited her friends to come and see the makeover of both herself and her apartment. Her friends asked me to design their hair after seeing hers. This provided a little income for me. I went to garage sales and bought old, discarded jewelry to strip down to bare components and create new designs. I painted shoes from a clearance rack at a discount store. I made scarves and added paint and beads. Quickly, I had a little boutique for people to shop in as I did hair. With the money I made, I bought Winnie a new TV. She was thrilled, and I felt wonderful to be able to give it to her. It lessened the shame of homelessness that hung over me.

Winnie and I decided go to Dad's in Minnesota. As soon as we arrived, we went for a walk to the park. Winnie got high, and I chain-smoked cigarettes. We were walking home, up a little hill, when suddenly I slipped and fell. I fell in slow motion, trying to catch myself. I came crashing down on wet leaves and slid on my chest down the pavement. It felt as if something had pushed me down. I heard a snapping sound and felt my hand break, and I instantly broke out in a sweat. I felt hot, dizzy, and nauseous. I had never broken a bone before, but I knew my hand was broken. I was wearing jeans, a sweater, and a jacket, but somehow I had scraped up my chest, hips, and arms even through my undergarments. When I moved my hand, it made strange, nauseating, cracking noises. Because of my lack of money, I didn't go to the hospital.

Early the next morning, Winnie and I were on Dad's front steps drinking coffee. Our dogs were with us. I was extremely sore from the fall. My broken hand was throbbing. Suddenly, and without warning, Winnie's dog growled and lunged at my face. In one split second, the dog laid my nose wide open. The bite split through cartilage and ripped my nose open from below my nostril up the entire length. Teeth marks had punctured my cheeks and nose. My glasses broke off my face. I bled intensely. Winnie had a look of complete horror and said, "Oh my God, Ada, it's really bad!" Without moving, she screamed for Dad. I was afraid and trying to calm my dog, who was also very frightened. Dad came out and just about fell over. The blood from a nose injury is, let's just say, abundant. I was sitting in a pool of it feeling dizzy.

Dad grabbed a bath towel, handed it to me, and ran back inside. I heard the attached garage door open. He started his car, backed out, and shouted to me to get in. I had already bled through the bath towel, and he handed me another one. I was afraid to look as the towels quickly began filling with blood. No one said anything as we sped to the emergency room.

Upon our arrival, staff raced me back to a room. They started an IV and injected my face to numb the pain. I wondered why they X-rayed my entire body and performed an MRI body scan. I lay still in this huge tube and thought it was a nightmare that I'd surely wake up from. I wondered if the fading bruises from Damien still showed. As they were taking the report from me, I realized they thought a dog had mauled me. The broken hand, skinned up body, bruised neck, and bloodshot eyes made it appear that I had been in a war. I felt like I *had* been in a war.

I remember the look on the nurse's face when I tried to explain my injuries to her. I told her that the neck bruising and bloodshot eyes were from my husband, who had tried to kill me. Then I told her that I had fallen the night before and broken my hand and skinned up my body. When I told her that my face was the only thing the dog had attacked, I started to cry. Tears suddenly flooded out, and I wept in that emergency room. The nurse welled up in tears too as she sat riveted with her iPad in her lap. She stood up, hugged me, and left without a word. I wondered if God left me too and why all these horrible things kept happening. I felt cursed.

I worried that without insurance, employment, or money, the hospital wouldn't treat me. The drugs dulled the pain and caused the bleeding to subside. I asked to use the restroom. When I walked in, I saw my refection the first time. It was horrible. I slid down the wall and sat on the floor in that bathroom feeling dizzy and faint. I begged God to help me. The doctor walked in and said they were not equipped to handle the severity of my facial injury. He said the ambulance would take me downtown where plastic surgeons would be waiting. All I could think about was the money I didn't have and asked Dad to drive me. The doctor explained how extremely important time was with facial injuries and subsequent scarring. They handed paperwork to me and called the hospital to let them know I was coming. He said they would be waiting.

It was a long drive and when we arrived, they were swamped with stabbings, shootings, and very sick people. They took the paperwork and told me to be seated, but every seat was full. I stood with my back against a wall, feeling dizzy and sick. Everyone stared at me and people asked to take pictures of my face. They all asked what had happened and then what kind of dog had attacked me. My life felt like a very bad dream.

My mind wandered as we waited and waited. I was preoccupied and thinking about a job interview I had finally arranged with a high-end salon in Minneapolis. If they hired me, the job would pay my medical bills and provide a way to survive. I wondered what my face would look like in a couple of days for the interview. I wondered if it would ever be the same or if I would be permanently disfigured. After an hour of waiting, the pain intensified. My entire body hurt. I asked how long it would be as the nurse looked up at me with disdain. They put me in a room and shot me full of more pain medication. I waited for almost four more hours before anyone came in. The dog attack had occurred almost eight hours ago.

Finally a doctor walked in. He looked shocked at the condition of my face and said, "Because you waited so long to come in, I don't think we'll be able to save the end of your nose. It's necrotic, and I believe it'll have to be removed." He went on to say, "You can have plastic surgery sometime in the future to try and correct the disfigurement you will have. Today, we will try to save as much as we can." I almost started to laugh even though inside I wanted to die. I calmly told him I'd been waiting all day. Then I looked him in the eyes and told that doctor everything. I told him about my husband, the fall, the dog, the first hospital, and the five hours I'd been at his hospital. I didn't shed a tear until he began to cry. Then I joined him.

He hugged me and told me this was the day old residents went out and new ones came on. I would learn that Dr. Johnson was a dental student doing his last day of a residency in the ER. He said they were extremely busy, and there would be a long wait for an operating room and a plastic surgeon. I wondered if this was the case because I did not have insurance. Dr. Johnson said that if I trusted him and signed a release form, he would do what he could surgically in that little room. Before I could answer, Dr. Johnson said it would be just him and me and that he wouldn't even have a nurse assist. I said, "Do it."

In a calm, peaceful voice, he asked me to please call him Gabriel as he gently went to work on my face. Gabriel was kind, soft-spoken, and had very warm brown eyes. He calmed me immediately. Gabriel talked to me about his school, graduating, and beginning his new life as he carefully worked on my face. He told me his faith had gotten him through. After a few minutes, he asked for my permission to take pictures during and after the surgery for a final paper he was writing. I thought it was funny to have this young guy whipping out an iPhone and snapping pictures as he operated on my nose. I had seventy-five stitches in my face, cartilage completely reformed into new nostrils, and tubes to breathe out of when he was finished. Also, I still had all of my nose intact.

Gabriel showed me how the darkened skin was beginning to blush in pinklike colors. He said I would be doing all of my follow-up care with his dental college and that although he was graduating, he wanted to keep in touch to make sure everything was healing as he had prayed for. Gabriel also said he was going to do his very best to see that I was not charged for any follow-up care. Not charged? God was in this. Even now He was with me. He had heard my plea on the bathroom floor early that morning. Abba had sent an angel named Gabriel, disguised as a dental student, to help. It was late when we were finally back at Dad's house. Even with meds, the pain was intense. I looked in the mirror through what was left of my glasses and was grateful that my eyes were only bruised. A couple of days later, I was sipping coffee when a sudden pain shot through my front teeth as they cracked off into my coffee cup. The impact of the dog attack had cracked them. I cried silent tears. My spirit was very down and my soul ached. I felt totally defeated and so ugly. God had just shown me that He was with me, yet I felt so defeated and ashamed for feeling down and ugly. I was sad and didn't have any fight left. In a matter of a few weeks, I had become homeless, carless, had seventy-five stitches in my face, broken teeth, a broken hand, was black and blue everywhere, but mostly I was black and blue in my heart. I felt like I was dying. Two days later, I went to the job interview anyway. They stared at me in horror and disbelief. My desperation was obvious and didn't match the reputation I had in the industry. They didn't offer me a position.

That was the beginning of many rejections. I applied everywhere for any kind of work without a single offer. After the stitches were removed, we went back to Winnie's. Dad offered me a low interest loan to help me repair my teeth. Gabriel had deeply blessed me. I was not billed for any of his services to repair my face or any of the treatments I received for follow-up appointments at the college. I've never had plastic surgery, and I didn't lose the end of my nose. I breathe normally. I can smell normally. The scarring is minimal, considering the trauma.

Through it all God was with me. He'd never once let me down. I clung to Him and I just kept walking. I kept putting one foot in front of the other and trusting God. Julian gave me the will to live, and it was God's outstretched hand I reached for. On days my head hung low, I would find Jesus around the corner waiting to lift my chin and my spirits with unsuspected blessings, like Gabriel, to help me through. In a matter of weeks I had been become unrecognizable even to myself.

 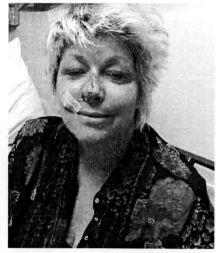

Cold Hard Facts

The word is a lamp unto my feet, a light on my path.
Psalm 119:105

Winnie was never home. I spent my days combing the Internet looking for any kind of work. My entire world was wrapped up tightly in fear. Damien was still calling me constantly. The messages were very scary and bizarre. Sometimes he threatened to "hunt me down." Other times he wanted to meet for a romantic weekend. He asked me to meet him in Chicago, Michigan, and Toronto. He actually said we needed to meet where no one would ever find us so we could reunite and fix our marriage. He begged me to go to a resort in Lake Geneva and Mackinac Island for a reunion weekend! Damien had zero conscience, and his delusion terrified me.

One day, I noticed a man sitting in a car staring up at my window. He had Wisconsin license plates. He saw me looking out at him, and he made a phone call before he sped away. I feared that Damien had hired that man to locate me. My fear was primal and constant. I called the police to report the man but hung up feeling ridiculous. I was trying to explain why I feared the mystery man in the car—a car that had already sped away and that I hadn't had the right mind to even write down the license plate number for. I was so afraid. The police called me back and instead of asking for help, I assured them that I was mistaken. My fear paralyzed me.

The next morning, I called a local shelter for advice. I couldn't take the constant harassment and fear I was living in. I spoke to a man named Michael. Immediately, he tried to get me to come to the shelter and even offered to have me picked up. I refused. Michael spent many hours on the phone with me. He asked detailed questions and listened closely to my responses. Many times, my answers led him to probe deeper. Then he asked me a series of questions and wanted me to answer with yes or no. After several hours, he asked if I knew what a sociopath was and guided me to a website with 150 questions concerning sociopaths. There I found the same questions he had been asking me. He told me that he had asked me the same questions in several ways, and my answers were always the same. He had scored my answers.

A score of 75 percent meant you were dealing with a sociopath. All—100 percent—of the answers I gave Michael showed that Damien was a sociopath. I asked Michael to define "sociopath." Before he answered, Michael asked if Damien had ever threatened to strangle me before he'd attempted to kill me. I told him that Damien had choked me in an intimate moment but that he was very remorseful. Michael said, "Damien wasn't remorseful, he was practicing!" My knees buckled as I sat down, stomach in knots, as Michael went on.

Michael told me that strangling a victim is a deeply personal murder. The word "murder" shot terror into my heart. He went on to spoon-feed me cold, hard facts. Domestic violence murders can be characterized by sudden murders like a stabbing or a shooting in a rage and in an instant. Strangulation is different, Michael said. The killer finds satisfaction in looking straight into the eyes of his victim as he chokes the life out of them. It's a deeply personal killing. Michael continued explaining to me that a sociopath playacts, practices, and plots and plans before he strikes. As Michael spoke, deep fear and panic settled into me. Damien had planned this and practiced!

As he continued, Michael went on to explain that many times sociopaths have very little or no conscience. They are charming and in most cases, very smart. Most sociopaths are incapable of experiencing love outside of loving themselves. Due to a lack of conscience and remorse, they don't learn from their mistakes but rather act out more intensely over time to accomplish their self-motivated goals. They isolate themselves and their victims. They can be prone to alcohol and drug abuse. He explained the fine line between typical sociopath versus a psychopath's characteristics, saying a sociopath has very little conscience, is self-centered, and self-motivated. A psychopath has zero conscience and will do anything to accomplish his self-centered and self-motivated actions. A sociopath may only fantasize about killing; a psychopath will strike with no empathy or conscience.

This knowledge Michael force-fed me settled unspeakable fear deep into my soul. I asked Michael what I should do. He told me I needed to stop running and to go to the police right away. He said I was in danger and that I needed to take it very seriously. He told me he'd made a full report, an audio recording and file, and was turning it into the police. He said he had to by law. Michael told me I needed to get a no-contact order immediately but also warned me to put no trust in it.

Michael said many women make the mistake of letting their guard down with a false sense of security when they have a court order in their hands. He said it could make Damien angrier, but it was the much-needed start of paperwork I would need to have him arrested WHEN he came after me again. He said very seldom do these men stop until they are fully exposed publicly. The reality of everything was settling in. I went into almost an autopilot mode. I felt numb, scared, and extremely alone. Very methodically, I had been isolated from many people I knew with the exception of Damien's family. His family had vanished quickly.

I wondered if I'd live through this or if Damien would be successful and kill me. His calls, texts, and emails continued. He begged for forgiveness and a reunion. When I did not respond, he would lash out in severe hatred and anger. As deep fear engulfed me, it got to the point that I was afraid to close the shower curtain. I barely slept at night and continued to push myself with caffeine and cigarettes.

Winnie was served an eviction notice and spun deeper into depression. As I packed for her, she lashed out at me in anger. I was growing resentful, and she continued with depressed sarcasm about how she would rather be dead than move. There was no place for her to go, so together we went back to Dad's.

For He shall give His angels charge
over you and to keep you safe in all your ways.
Psalm 91:11

I prayed we'd make it to Minnesota without any problems. As I pumped gas into the truck, Damien texted, "Drive safely." The constant terror of wondering if he was watching me or having me followed made my stomach ache and my heart grow very weary. I was growing to know fear and evil as my new reality. The constant awareness that I was being stalked loomed over me and snatched my sleep away at night. I thought about how vulnerable I was and wondered if I was putting Winnie's or Dad's life at risk.

We stopped for food before getting onto the freeway. While I was standing in line, Damien texted me again, this time asking for Dad's Social Security number. He said he needed it immediately and that, "With it, I can handle everything." I wondered what everything was and like always, didn't respond. Damien told me he knew exactly where I was in Cedar Rapids, Iowa, and knew I was returning to Dad's. If I could have just lain down and died at that moment, I would have. Winnie was nervous when I showed her the text. God gave me peace as we silently got into the truck together and set out for Minnesota.

I lived in a state of heightened awareness of every sound, smell, and movement around me. One day in a Target bathroom, I suddenly smelled insulin. I almost screamed as I ran out of the public restroom in fear. That smell took me instantly back to Damien pacing around that room with his needle threatening me. Everywhere I went, I looked over my shoulder. Each time Damien would threaten me, I'd take the information to the police department and file another report. Although I was doing exactly as I was told to do by every DV counselor and policeman I'd encountered, my fear deepened. They said all that I was doing was necessary for my safety, but it always left me feeling more vulnerable. I wondered if each legal step I took was only making Damien angrier. Many events occurred leading up to a court date being set for my request for a restraining order.

I learned that Damien had been stalking me long before I ever met him. In learning this, I also had to face the fact that Damien had never loved me. He had simply hunted me. This was extremely difficult for me to comprehend. It absolutely crushed me, broke my heart, and brought me a solidified feeling of shame and complete unworthiness. Ugliness blanketed me. I had faced a lot of rejection in my life until I met Damien. He had made me feel loved, cherished, appreciated, and needed. Now I knew none of those things had ever existed beyond my own delusion. Rejection lodged deeply into my soul.

One of the first times Damien found me, he had used the GPS in my phone. I didn't know that technology existed or that he was viewing my account online. Software coupled with a phone GPS had provided him my exact location. I had been having trouble accessing my account and had decided to go into the local cell phone store for help. There, I had seen my account passwords appear to change right before my eyes as I tried to explain to the Verizon store manager why I had come to the store. As we looked at my account log, I had discovered it showed activities I had nothing to do with. Then suddenly, an outside source had locked us out of my account. The store manager had listened closely when I explained my safety was at stake.

Like me, watching my account being highjacked before his own eyes had scared the manager. I had explained the danger and insisted on having a guarantee of privacy for my account before I left that store. The manager called his corporate office and then the police department. The police came into the store and took statements from both of us. The Minneapolis police were beginning to know me by name. They were kind and always encouraged me to call if I even suspected Damien was near. Although their recognition of the danger I was in brought me much needed help, it also heightened my fear. I kept hoping I'd wake up from the nightmare that was now my life.

I spent many nights at the police station as Damien continued to stalk me relentlessly. Somehow, he seemed to always know where I was. The frantic trips to the police station and the constant fear were exhausting and debilitating. Life felt like a stage, and I was an actress wearing someone else's mask. My entire self-worth and identity had been stripped away.

In my life, I've had plenty of money and I can tell you for certain that it doesn't buy happiness. However, I can also tell you for certain that a complete lack of money will make you miserable. I was desperate. With money, I could buy a car. A car would allow me to find more work and the freedom I needed to survive. I found my wedding rings in a dresser and decided to sell them on Craigslist. Emails came in immediately through a secured Craigslist email. One young couple seeking the rings seemed perfect. They provided a Minneapolis phone number. They were newlyweds and very excited.

I felt good knowing this couple would find joy in the rings. I was thrilled to get rid of them and have the much-needed cash. I asked to meet them right away at a specific area outside of the Mall of America. Damien was many hours away in Milwaukee, so meeting right away would ensure my safety.

I chose the Mall of America because it is big, very well patrolled, and always has lots of people walking around. I pulled in a few minutes late after a freeway backup. Just before I arrived, my phone rang. A Wisconsin area code flashed on the screen. I picked up the phone, and before I could even decide if I would speak, an impatient voice on the other end said he was waiting! It was not the voice of the young man I'd spoken with. I apologized and said I'd changed my mind. That caller became irate and began yelling at me. I hung up without saying a word and drove straight to the police station.

Before I got to the station, Damien called me and left message after message. He shouted that I was discarding him like garbage. He shouted that I had lowered myself to even trying to "liquidate my ring," which he said was a very expensive gift and token of his love. In his rage, he exposed his scheme to find me. I filed another police report and listened to a female officer talk about how dangerous it is to sell anything on Craigslist. That night she called me and told me that Damien had contacted her. He had been crying and asking for advice. He'd told her that he loved me and was worried about me because I was mentally unstable.

Damien continued to torment me with messages telling me he knew my location, and he sometimes confirmed it as he spoke. I felt like a hunted animal. I was terrified to have the lights on at night for fear he'd be looking in. Dad had no window coverings of any kind on his large picture window in the front of his home. The big, beautiful blue spruce outside gave him all the privacy he needed from neighbors, but it left me feeling like I had a target on my head. I sat in his basement in the dark and in fear of the darkness in the house *and* in my soul.

I spent countless hours numbly filing reports at the police station. I always brought documentation substantiating everything I said. Damien continued to stalk me and grew angrier as time went on. His emails and messages became more threatening. The police began to insist that I file a restraining order. To obtain one, I'd have to see Damien in court. I knew it wouldn't deter him, and I feared it would make things worse.

Everywhere I turned, Damien was conning people. He was smart, articulate, charming, and very convincing. He also has zero filters and no conscience. Damien contacted people who were close to me without batting an eye. Damien and a man claiming to be his attorney called Dad and Gee. His sister Lind called to beg my father for information about me. He emailed Dad, Gee, and Justo. The most startling and truly shocking event was when he even managed to con my divorce attorney!

When I finally had the money saved to file for divorce, I learned that I had to file in Wisconsin. It felt like another slap in my face. I found an attorney who specialized in helping women, specifically in DV cases. She was compassionate and experienced with DV, although I never thought she grasped the financial devastation Damien had caused. She told me that my divorce would be inexpensive, simple, and fast. She encouraged me to pursue legal action with the state against him for the violence and to research where the money had gone. With a sense of hope, I signed paperwork and gave her all the money I had with the promise of a fast divorce, then I returned to Minneapolis.

A few months later, the court date arrived. The legal advocates at the shelter in Minneapolis made safety arrangements for me. The Milwaukee police would escort me from the parking garage to the courtroom. I will never forget stepping off the elevator with the police officer by my side and seeing my attorney sitting, laughing, and chatting with Damien! She knew everything, and there she sat. The police officer put his arm around me tightly and told me not to look at them and that he would walk me straight into the courtroom and stay with me the entire time. I knew God had sent another angel for me. This angel was big and strong and was dressed in a police uniform.

My attorney left Damien in the lobby and approached where I was sitting with the police officer. As she stood, she very matter-of-factly said she'd gotten to know Damien better. She said he'd come into her office and expressed how deeply in love with me he was. She said she could see he was very remorseful and truly in love with me. She suggested we all cancel the divorce hearing and go to her office along with Damien and talk together with "cooler heads." She said Damien even offered to take us both out to lunch. I felt sick, and my ears rang. The policeman walked me back to my car after I fired her and postponed the divorce court date. Damien laughed at my back as I left and shouted to me that I would "have another birthday and spend a fortune, and I will still be your husband." Damien could charm and convince anyone of anything.

As the threats escalated, the police and the shelter pushed me to file for a restraining order. I visited the courthouse to ask questions about the process. I was told that I first had to apply for the order. The woman behind the counter explained that restraining orders were issued for thirty, sixty, or ninety days depending on the judge's decision. As she spoke, I kept imagining Damien storming the courthouse with a gun. It seemed pointless to me. As I numbly filled out paperwork, I knew he wouldn't be deterred and I feared he might become angrier.

The night before court, in my dreams I was seeing myself being shot before I even entered the building. I arrived two hours early and sprinted to the doors. The shelter told me an advocate named Susan would be there waiting for me. As I rushed into the heavy front doors, there Susan was.

Susan was soft-spoken, motherly, and calmed me immediately. She assured me that I was going to be okay. She told me to not look at Damien but to keep my eyes on the judge. She told me to look straight into the judge's eyes and to answer every single question slowly and with as much detail as I could remember. The shelter had been happy that a particular judge had been assigned to my case. However, at the courthouse, I noticed that the name outside the courtroom was different than the name of the judge I thought I had been assigned. I asked Susan about the apparent change. She said that the man assigned to my case was out for personal reasons and a new judge had been pulled in. Susan didn't mask her unhappiness about this. She said our new judge was a woman, Judge Miller, and had a reputation for being very tough on women.

We were in the courtroom for over an hour when Damien and his lawyer arrived. Susan let me know he was there, and she held my hand. I did exactly as Susan had directed me to and stared at the empty bench. As strange as it sounds, I could smell Damien. His cologne with a faint smell of insulin sickened me. My heart was pounding so hard I felt like my shirt moved with every heartbeat. Damien called to me, and I didn't move. He called louder, and I remained stoic. I stared at the bench as the judge came in and we all stood. I looked only straight into the judge's eyes as Susan had told me to do. Even when she was talking to Damien or his lawyer, I stared at Judge Miller, clutching Susan's hand.

I answered every question slowly. As I gave details, I tried to not let any emotion show. I offered certified documentation for every accusation I made. I had legally certified transcriptions of every text, email, and voice mail Damien had sent. Police reports from multiple states in my stack of paperwork rose six inches high.

As I answered all of Judge Miller's questions slowly and offered supporting documentation, she only looked at some of it. My stack looked like a pillow with yellow and pink fringe around the edges. Everything was labeled with post-its. The post-its extended off the page. Because there were so many of them, wrapping them around the entire border made it easier for me to access information quickly. I had placed everything in chronological order and labeled it all with a date and subject. I had rehearsed this at home in an effort to quickly provide everything needed for any question the judge would ask.

Damien began panicking and interrupted. He said I was out of my mind and that my statements were not true. Damien's attorney asked to see several of the documents. As he looked at them, Damien began to cry and begged me to "come home." He wailed that he loved me and would spend the rest of his life "proving it to me." His attorney requested to meet with Susan and me privately. Judge Miller agreed and had a bailiff stay with Damien.

We all stepped into a private conference room just outside the courtroom. Damien's attorney asked to see all of my documentation. As he began to leaf through it, he saw where I'd highlighted every single threat and many bizarre sexual statements. Very quickly he could see that Damien was lying, not me. Damien's attorney handed me a letter Damien had written to him explaining my "mental condition." Damien had brutally lied about me. His attorney stood up, shook my hand, and wished me safety. He left a page of the letter Damien had written on the table. As he talked with Damien, I could see Damien's anger and they began arguing.

Susan held my hand, and I nervously stared at Judge Miller's empty bench. Damien pleaded for me to look at him. He begged me to "come home" again. The judge returned and as we stood, Damien sobbed and told Judge Miller that I was "the love of his life." As we all sat down, Damien's attorney stood back up abruptly and said they'd agree to the restraining order, no contest. In response, Judge Miller asked to see the paperwork I'd provided and she left for her chambers with every single CD, photo, and all my other documentation. When she returned, she didn't issue the restraining order for thirty, sixty, or ninety days. She issued a full-blown order of protection for not only me but for Julian. It exceeded the US borders for the maximum allowed time in Minnesota: two years. Susan held my hand the entire time. She squeezed it tightly when Judge Miller announced her decision.

Judge Miller had Damien escorted to another room and asked that the bailiff remain with him. She told me she would hold Damien for one hour to give me plenty of time to leave safely. She also told me that based on what she knew, I could proceed with the state to have him arrested. Judge Miller said she'd received copies of my file from Michael at a Cedar Rapids shelter and she handed me copies. Michael was another gift from God. He was another angel on my path. Michael was still helping me.

Judge Miller told me that Damien would be found guilty on all counts. She also cautioned that typically crimes of this nature resulted in very little time served. Judge Miller warned that the real danger would follow after his release. She cautioned me, saying that moving forward legally against him would tie me up in court for at least two years as a key witness for the state. She asked me to consider what was most important to me: revenge or safety and a new start. My ears started to ring, and I felt tears well up in my eyes when Judge Miller advised me to change my name and to present a request to the State of Iowa to have a complete new birth certificate issued. She said I should consider applying for a new Social Security number.

I did not feel a single shred of the desire for revenge, only the desire to be safe. Why was it that a judge granting me all of this protection and then turning around with these other suggestions made my fear grow deeper? I walked in seeking protection and had been granted far more than I had asked for. But I was leaving with a heightened fear. I realized that even through the fear, I had tried to downplay the events that had brought me to this point. The severity of my life, my safety, and my future as I knew it stunned me. Although I left the courthouse with the maximum possible order of protection, I was terrified.

Susan walked me out with her arm around me. She was tearful and said she'd never experienced a day like that. She told me she had been advocating for women for many years and had never seen a judge take such a long time and dig so deeply to protect someone on a first offense and particularly when most of the events and addresses listed were in a different state. Susan asked me if I understood how rare it was to have an order of protection for two years issued on a first complaint. She gave me a motherly smile and said she believed I must have angels with me. I told her I did and that God was with me. I told her God put an angel named Michael at a women's shelter in Iowa, and that He sent a second one dressed in a police uniform to accompany me in Milwaukee, and there was another angel that sat on the bench dressed as a judge that day.

The angel that sat right next to me, I told Susan, had held my hand through the entire event and had given me the courage to push through. I told her she was an angel that I'd never forget. Susan told me she'd never forget me. And there we stood, both in tears, in front of the Minneapolis courthouse. As we left, I knew I would never see her again. I thanked God for her and all the angels He puts amongst us.

In Not For

In everything give thanks
1 Thessalonians 5:16

The order of protection only magnified my world of primal fear. I was tired of running, of living in the heaviness. I was losing hope that life could ever be different. Darkness whispered deafening words of hatred in my ears. In my self-hate, I couldn't hear God. I wondered if I had imagined every moment I had with Him. Maybe I'd developed a coping mechanism to survive the horror of my world. That dark voice whispered to me that only an extremely self-centered person would think God, the creator of the universe, would listen to them personally. I felt crushed, spiritually compressed, into an unredeemable pile of nothingness.

I spent my days combing the Internet looking for any kind of work. No one wanted to employ me. I wondered if my scarred face was scaring them off. Unemployment deepened my self-hatred.

Lying in bed one night, I thought about the push, ambition, and very hard work it had taken to establish myself as a successful business owner. A high school dropout and runaway had evolved into a successful entrepreneur, something that had taken determination and guts. It had taken moxie. I decided to treat my life as a start-up business. The drive I needed was laser sharp when I focused on Julian. He gave me the will to survive.

Instead of looking for a job, I started drumming up business everywhere I went. I sold my art and designed hair in people's homes. I used discarded jewelry for components to create new pieces. The smallest baby steps, like creating and selling one necklace, were now monumental. Retail and art were second nature to me in the business world when cases and cases of new goods streamed in weekly. Now, with only two or three necklaces at a time, I began earning and saving money. In a few months, I managed to save enough to buy a car.

Julian came for Christmas! Having my boy "home" filled me with almost uncontainable joy. The three days we spent together brought me the courage I needed to keep pushing through. Julian left the day after Christmas, and police called later that day with devastating news. Damien had been ticketed for speeding near Dad's house, 350 miles from where Damien lived. This news was a dreaded confirmation that Damien was still stalking me relentlessly, even on Christmas day.

My fear and the fear my presence brought to others everywhere I went—the heaviness and the shame—were just too much. I saw fear in the faces of everyone, everywhere. No one wanted to be around me. Dad confided to me that he had begun sleeping with a gun under his pillow even when I wasn't there, "just in case." It shocked me but made me understand how he felt. I was numb, but others were not. My God, how had my life come to this? Dad's neighbors questioned me, wondering if the gossip was true. I had brought fear to his neighborhood. I wished I could disappear.

I was deeply depressed as I sat in the park in the freezing cold contemplating whether everyone would be better off if I was dead. I'm not sure where I got the courage, but I called my friend Jo. I hadn't spoken with Jo in several years. Numbly, I tried to explain what was happening in my life, and Jo instantly said, "Come now. Come stay with me! Can you get here, Ada? I will come to Minnesota for you if you can't." Instantly, Jo's love dissolved me into a puddle of tears on that park bench. She lived 350 miles away and in the same city as Damien. Jo is extremely important to me. I've loved and looked up to her for many years. Damien had manipulated circumstances and isolated me from her. Soon Jo and I would compare stories and have a deeper understanding of how a sociopath's mind works.

I loaded my life into my car, filled up the tank, and with the few bucks I had left to my name, I hit the road in blizzardlike conditions and somehow arrived in Milwaukee. Shame overtook me as I got closer, and I couldn't get myself to go to Jo's. I drove to a dark, abandoned church parking lot up high on a hill. I looked at all the beautiful Christmas lights over the city and thought of the families celebrating Christmas in those homes. Only a few short years ago, Mom, Dad, Julian, and I had celebrated Christmas in our home. I thought of the

145

warmth and love we had then and how I'd never imagined it could end. My heart broke thinking about Julian and the terrible mom I'd become. All I'd ever wanted was to be the best mom possible for him and Justine. My heart felt like it was in a million unrepairable pieces. Darkness convinced me that Julian would be better off if I was dead.

Darkness told me it could look like an accident, and Julian would be okay. He'd get through it. Darkness whispered to me that he'd be better off without the shame of me. Darkness reminded me that no one else in the world cared if I died. I was Googling carbon monoxide poisoning and how people die in cars. I was planning my death.

I distinctly heard, "In all things give thanks." I'd heard this before, maybe in the Bible. If those were God's words, I was seriously selfish because I didn't feel grateful for the disaster my life had become. I wondered if God was punishing me. I Googled those words to see if they really were from a Scripture. I found them and wondered if God had just spoken to me. 1 Thessalonians 5:16: "In all things give thanks." Suddenly I heard God say to me that the operative word is IN not FOR. He explained to me that He did not bring all this pain into my life and expect me to thank Him for it. No! That wasn't Him! He asked me to thank Him IN every circumstance! Why? Because He showed me that He'd never left me. He had always been with me in every single storm I'd been through. He showed me how He had saved my life over and over and over. God showed me the angels He'd planted as messengers, providers, and protectors.

Like a movie, my mind flashed through dark moments when I should've died but didn't. I flashed through the birth of Julian, the sudden emergency C-section and fear that he was going to die. God was with me every single minute. He showed me how he had held Julian, Dad, and me in His palm through the loss of Mom. I wept tears of gratitude. God explained to me that to thank Him meant to give Him praise.

He began to show me that to praise means to love Him in heavenly prayers and singing. God showed me that to praise is to worship Him in song completely abandoned to the world, just Him and me. He showed me that He wanted me to know and never again doubt that He was with me and was never, ever going to leave. God showed me that He is IN every detail of my life! And you know what? He's in every detail of your life too! Every joy and every hellish moment, He is there.

I did exactly as He'd instructed me to. I turned on the radio that snowy night, and I began to praise God, to sing. "Beautiful" was the first song that played. My face had barely healed from seventy-five stitches and broken teeth, my heart was battered and severely broken, and my spirit was weary, but in that dark, abandoned parking lot, God told me I was beautiful. His words came alive to me that night. He held me, and I cried and sang to Him. Hope began to bubble up inside of my broken heart again. Suddenly it was daybreak, and the chains that had bound my soul were broken. It was as if I had been shackled and in a prison and I'd walked out of that prison cell knowing He was leading me. I knew He was with me and He'd never left. That evening I went to Jo's home, and another chapter of healing began.

God had shown me that in this world we will all have trouble. We will have hurts and sometimes unthinkable pain. He had carried me through murder, rape, rejection, suicide, depression, oppression, divorce, the loss of my best friend and Mom, the loss of a child, the loss of my home, the loss of my perceived life, and even bankruptcy. It had staggered me and left me unable to breathe. But those of us who know Jesus have a powerful weapon that destroys anything that attempts to rise up against us. It crumbles the walls of any prison cell you find yourself in. It's called Praise. It's impossible to praise and be hopeless. It's impossible to praise and feel fear. For God is in the midst, and He demolishes anything that is not of Him. God is Love. He is Perfect Love and Perfect Love casts out all fear. Fear will tell you no one cares. He will tell you that forever He is there.

I've never stopped praising Him, and I never will. His promises are true. In all things give thanks, give praise. He will raise up that broken spirit within you. He will soothe your battered and abused soul. He will teach you the secrets of darkness. He will provide for you from the least expected places. He will protect you from all evil. He will build rivers in your desert. He will give you a future filled with hope and joy.

When I am made low,
He is made high

Jesus looked at them and said to them,
"With men this is impossible,
but with God all things are possible."
Matthew 19:26

With arms wide open, Jo welcomed me to her home. It was beautiful and full of art, color, creativity, and love. Here, there was no judgment, condemnation, or anger; there was only love. Jo walked me to her lower level overlooking the beautiful Milwaukee River. It was exactly like Jo: beautiful, serene, and peaceful. A beautiful bedroom beckoned with a big, soft bed and even softer piles of pillows. That room was filled with art, books, and a sense of light. A very wide window overlooked the river in front of the bed. An old cozy cottage sat on the river's edge on the other side. Huge leafless trees and lush evergreen pines filled the dark winter skies. They lined the shore and reflected on the river's smooth, icy surface. Jo's bedroom felt like a warm, welcoming hug.

Even Jo's bathroom was filled with her creativity. She told me to settle in, get comfortable, and the room was mine for as long as I needed it. Tears welled up in my eyes, but I held them back. I wanted to fall to my knees in gratitude. For the first time in a very long time, I felt safe. I felt no judgment, only protection and genuine concern. That night I slept like a baby for the first time in a very, very long time. Jo's bedroom would become a healing room saturated in tears, prayer, and hope.

Jo is a successful and very gifted artist who has inspired me for years. She shared her love of pulp and how to stretch boundaries to create huge dimensional sculptures. Over the years, we did figure drawing and monotype printing on handmade paper with Jo's huge press. What I found the next morning was different. She took me into a studio space just around the corner from the bedroom. Jo motioned to huge batches of pulp in five-gallon buckets. She'd just made them for me. She turned me loose with pulp, paint, and healing. She gave me a knowing smile and left me alone to create. In her basement studio I cried, prayed, created, and found peace again. It was profoundly healing and made me feel like maybe I was going to make it through. I cried creative tears of pure joy in that little basement studio.

Every night that Jo and her husband were home, they set a place for me at their table. There were always placemats and candles and laughter. They were so very kind and loving to me and to each other. After dinner, I'd go downstairs most nights. They always asked me to join them for a movie, but I was determined to not become a burden or interfere with their lives. Shame was starting to creep back in. Darkness shouted to me that I was a loser and a burden everywhere I went.

Every day I looked for work, and I spent the evenings in Jo's studio. The creative process brought me peace and helped me fight off anxiety. I found jewelry at garage sales and the Salvation Army. I searched for pieces of ribbon, gently used handbags, and wallets wherever I could. I tore apart the old jewelry and created new artful designs. Paint, beads, and pieces of silk became beautiful scarves. Paint, ribbons, and beads would upcycle the handbags into new artistic designs. I was slowly building a collection of women's accessories out of basically nothing. With Jo's prompting and the tiny bit of self-confidence she had restored in me, I took that collection to a local gallery. To my surprise, they loved it and took it all on consignment.

Within days of seeing my work in their front window, a major unplanned street construction began right in front of that gallery. A huge detour was required to access it. Business halted, and a phone call confirmed my fears: The owner had decided to close shop. I was so sad and recognized defeat in myself and that I no longer had the fighter spirit in me.

I continued a futile search for work. Another month went by in which I couldn't sleep. Heaviness, shame, and guilt wracked me again. One morning I overheard Jo's husband ask how long I would be there. I felt I had reached my limit and had become a burden to these wonderful people I'd grown to love. It deepened my heaviness. I thought about leaving all the time but didn't know where to turn or what to do. It was a bitter cold Wisconsin winter, so sleeping in my car wouldn't work. I left early every morning, but I'd run out of places to look for work and run out of the heart to continue. I'd stay in my car for as long as I could stand the cold. McDonald's had a promotion for one dollar large coffees. Every coffee came with a sticker on the side for free oatmeal. I had lived on coffee and oatmeal for a while in Minnesota, and it had become my staple again. I would leave early and not come back until late. I was grateful for the heated home and bed but felt like a burden to my beautiful friend Jo and her husband, and I hated myself for it.

Then one day a sudden and unexpected door opened for me at an upscale local grocery store. I could have never imagined I'd be so happy to have a job at a grocery store gift shop, but I was thrilled beyond measure. The owner of this local chain had been one of my clients. The manager, Mike, told me she had recognized me and had admired my shop. It was hard to believe it had only been a couple of years. It seemed like a lifetime ago that I'd had my business. I was told she was interested in having me design displays for all their stores and to assist her in buying for all the gift stores! I was grateful and very excited. I was determined to be the best possible employee. The black dress code was perfect for my hair-designer wardrobe. I was like a kid eager and nervous for the first day of school. I planned my outfit, laid it out, and had a hard time sleeping the night before. I arrived eager and a half hour early.

Within minutes of my arrival, Rachel, the floral manager who also filled in as the gift store manager, took me into the back office. She told me that she didn't care what the owner saw in me, and that I worked for her. She told me that I dressed too fancy, my hair was too styled, and that I shouldn't wear any makeup to her store. Rachel told me that I wouldn't be creating displays, she wanted me to paint walls. Rachel didn't mean mural work, but to change the wall color from white to yellow. Sternly, she instructed me to go across the street and buy yellow paint. I smiled and turned to grab my keys. Rachel shot me her first smile and told me that I wasn't allowed to drive on store time. I felt the laughter behind my back as I trudged through the slop and snow, across the parking lot and busy six-lane road and back again with the bucket of paint. I was happy to have work and determined to make her like me. I painted carefully, trying not to ruin my outfit. I saw her smirking with a few others in the distance.

Mike arrived and welcomed me with a big smile and a bigger hug. He said that they were eager to see my work displaying the new spring merchandise. I wondered if he had noticed that the walls of the gift shop were a different color or if he knew I had just painted them. Rachel walked away in an obvious huff.

I was excited to dive in. Cases of brightly colored spring gift items, artsy gift bags, bows, and boxes summoned me. So did candles, flowers, funky dishes, brightly colored kitchen gadgets, flowerpots, novelty napkins, huge painted umbrellas, cookbooks, and Easter decor in bright springy colors. As I unpacked those boxes, I began to "see" just like I had in my own stores. I used a little forklift and pulled chairs and props and display pieces from the back staging area. Brightly colored chairs sat around two center tables. I put them on top of the tables and each other to create an eye-catching stage for the new spring items.

People from other departments began stopping by as I arranged new merchandise in unique and very creative ways. I was in my element now and implementing design techniques that had always been successful in driving sales for my businesses. Rachel watched me closely with her hands on her hips as I climbed the ladder and hung umbrellas upside down from a monofilament line suspended from the rafters. She questioned my every move, but she also let me continue. The new merchandise was selling off that table as I created. I was relieved when Rachel left for the day. Even though I could see she didn't like me, I felt that if I just kept being kind she would see me for who I was. I trusted that she would recognize I was on her team. I went to Jo's after that long workday and felt grateful and relieved and like perhaps I'd found a creative niche and a much needed financial lifeline. That night, I looked at small studio apartments online and dreamed of independence.

The next day, Rachel was off and the store was very busy. We sold out of all of the new merchandise! The other store department managers were buzzing about it. It was thrilling, and I thanked God for the chance He was giving me.

I began an hour before Rachel's shift began the following day. When she arrived she took me to a back office right away. I thought maybe I'd won her over with great sales, but that wasn't the case. Rachel told me she was firing me. I was stunned and asked her why. She thought I hadn't put out all the new merchandise as she'd asked. I smiled and told her I had but that it had all sold. She rolled her eyes and said that was impossible. She began pulling up information on her computer that sat between us. Her face reddened as she saw that I indeed had told the truth. She wasn't happy. Instead she stormed out of the office angry and told me to stay there. In a matter of seconds, Rachel returned with Mike. She walked out and left me with him. Mike told me my constant disrespect for Rachel was inexcusable. He said she was a longtime employee and like part of their family. I tried to explain, but Mike put his hand up and did not want to hear anything. He slid paperwork across the desk for me to sign. He had just fired me.

I gathered my things and again felt every eye on my back as I left trying to hold back tears. I felt humiliated, rejected, and as low as I'd ever felt. After so many months trying to find work, I was fired before I'd even received my first paycheck. I drove back to the same church parking lot and cried in that little cold car. I didn't know how to face Jo and her husband or how to explain. The rest of that day and into the evening I spent in my car again in that abandoned church parking lot wallowing in sorrow, embarrassment, and shame. Rejection was as familiar as a Siamese twin. Rejection was an engrafted part of me now.

God came to me, and He calmed me. He told me that only in my weakness is He strong. God began showing me how I had tried to be the strength in my family my entire life. He showed me page by page how I had tried to be the strength, even as a little girl. I was the strength and had pushed to strive hard and succeed with Scott in my first marriage. I was the strength, motivator, and financial supplier in my marriage to Justo. I tried desperately to be the strength and glue for Justine and Julian. I had succeeded in none of these things. God showed me how I had been a confidante to my precious Mom. He showed me how I had tried to be a strong shoulder for everyone during Mom's battle with cancer. I had held Mom's hand as she died, and she had dried my tears. God showed me how I had been the strength and driving force in my business. He said I was always the strength in my relationships.

I didn't understand fully what God was saying, and I felt punished and ashamed. Slowly, I began to understand that my pride was being broken. He wanted me to run to Him and only Him, not my own strength. He showed me He had always been my Abba, my daddy. He showed me that His strength shows brightest when no one else can take credit or share in His glory. God told me that He would raise me up in His time and His way and it would be a new way, a new life and as He intended for it to be all along. He told me to trust Him. I wanted to lean fully on Him and trust. I cried out to Him that I had tried but fear always took over. I told Him I was so scared and that I felt separated and abandoned from my entire world. After almost a year, I was still homeless, jobless, and very scared. I felt judged everywhere I went, like a misfit. God assured me that He was not the one speaking those words or giving me those thoughts. He told me to trust Him. Then He was silent.

One day I received an email about an upcoming course in Iowa I dreamed of attending. I'd taken the first part and was profoundly blessed by it and the awesome people I'd met through it. It was expensive, far away, and impossible. I prayed myself to sleep that night, and God reminded me that He worked in impossibilities. I woke up to an email congratulating me on the full scholarship I'd received! I told Jo, and she shared in my excitement. Maybe I would find answers in Iowa.

Miracles in Iowa

And my God will meet All your needs
according to the riches of His glory in Christ Jesus.
Philippians 4:19

I crawled out of bed early that morning and knew deep inside that it would be the last time I woke up in that beautiful, peaceful Wisconsin bedroom. God had been speaking to me as I slept. He had told me that things were going to change and to trust Him. I knew this chapter in my life of the comfort and security, place of creativity, and zero judgment that Jo was giving me was closing. It seemed as if a season had suddenly passed by overnight. God had prepared me to step out in faith and complete trust in Him, to the unknown and in unwavering obedience again. He had tauaght me to hear His voice, to trust Him, and follow where He led.

Instead of preparing for a weekend in Iowa, I knew God was moving me again. But I didn't know where. There was a familiar comfort in the uneasiness of the unknown, because I knew it was Him. It was like a restful peace in the middle of a pending storm. I knew God was in charge and He would never let me down.

I planned to go see my cousin Andrew and his wife, Jamie, for the evening in Waterloo, Iowa, and then head to Iowa City.

I'd reconnected with Jamie, Andrew and his dad, my uncle Dennis, when I was with Winnie in Cedar Rapids. Dennis once was a very important part of my life, but divorce had separated him from our family decades before. Dennis called me and said he'd heard I was coming to Iowa. I've often wondered if he was behind that scholarship. If he was, he's never told me. Dennis said Jamie loved my art and had shown him my things online. Dennis said he would like to host an art open house for me at his home the night before the classes began. He said he had many friends eager to come to see my art. Dennis also invited me to stay at his home along with Pippy, his niece who was also attending the course. Every single need and far beyond what I could have imagined was provided for—again! God is so very awesome. I will always be amazed at how intimately He cares for me. Overnight there was provision again. Through Dennis, Abba was providing for me.

Jo and her husband left very early in the morning for a weekend trip. We'd said our goodbyes the night before, and I had planned to be gone for no more than a week when we parted. But that morning, God was telling me something different. In the back of my car, I packed up all the art I had and enough personal things to get by. Once again, I stepped out in faith and this time I set out for Iowa.

Deep inside, I knew He was leading me out of Wisconsin for the last time. I had a peace, truly a peace that surpasses all understanding knowing that I wasn't going to return. As I pulled out of Jo's driveway, tears rolled down my face in profound gratitude for the healing He had given me through Jo and her husband. I'd arrived at their home to be greeted with open arms. I had been broken, battered, and terrified. I was leaving strengthened in my spirit and with creativity reignited in my soul.

Jamie called as I drove and told me she had a coupon for a free night at a new casino hotel near their home. She said they'd never use it and would like me to enjoy it. The notion of having a comfy bed in a place all to myself was exciting and inviting, but still slightly scary. If I allowed it, darkness reminded me I was being stalked. I met Andrew and Jamie before going to the hotel. It was beautiful! My room had a white, fluffy, amazing king-size bed. A huge tub beckoned from the center of the room, and a soft white robe waited. All sorts of things to eat and drink were arranged artistically on the table in front of a sheer-covered window. That night, I truly felt like a princess. I slept soundly and with no fear. I didn't want the retreat to end. I took my time getting ready the next morning and left feeling alive, happy, and refreshed.

I noticed a coupon propped up against the desk lamp. It was for a complementary coffee at the gift store in the lobby. I wandered down and ordered a latte. As I stood there waiting for my coffee, I felt like a spotlight was shining on me. Every person working there, standing there, shopping there, or waiting on their coffees started noticing my painted boots, purse, and jewelry. I mean everyone! A woman from behind

the register came up to me and asked what brand my boots and purse were. Her name tag said "Judy, General Manager," and I explained that I was an artist and they were my creations. Judy asked if I offered wholesale pricing. Stammering just a little, I said, "Yes, of course!" I felt a nudge from God, and I mentioned that I had samples in my car. Judy's eyes lit up when I shared that I had jewelry, scarves, purses, wallets, and shoes, and she insisted that I bring in everything I had. God was on the move! I felt His spirit pushing me to have more confidence in my creations because really they were His creations.

I moved my car to the front where a bellhop could help me. The back of that car was packed full of my creations in paper grocery bags. I filled up a hotel cart and carefully wheeled it inside. To my surprise, the lobby was no longer empty. A huge, long line three or four people wide had formed the length of the entire lobby. They were waiting for an all-you-can-eat brunch buffet to open in fifteen minutes. They actually had to step aside to allow me to get through.

I soon realized they were shoppers, and not just any shoppers. God had planted them here. The gift shop also had grown very busy filled with people taking turns shopping and standing in line. Judy was busy helping customers, so I decided to put my creativity and years of retail experience to work. A line of tall pub-style tables with no chairs were lined up outside the store. I set up little displays on each table. I coordinated hand-painted boots, purses, and matching wallets with colorful scarves and jewelry on every table. Women started stepping out of the line and gathered around my tables asking to buy.

Judy came out with a look of confusion when she saw the women going bonkers over my things. I smiled at her. As she grinned back at me, I could not wipe the pure joy off my face. I felt validation and acceptance. I wondered what they'd all think if they knew I was a homeless lady with her life in the back of a car. Judy left saying she'd be right back. She returned carrying a huge stack of paperwork. She asked me to fill it out to be reviewed by their board, who made all retail decisions. My heart sunk as I glanced at it, and I bit my lower lip. It seemed impossible. The second line asked for an address. I didn't have an address.

Meanwhile, the women in line began asking for prices and pulling out their wallets. They offered to go to the ATMs in the casino to get cash and elbowed each other to keep a hand on the treasure they wanted from my tables. I looked at Judy without saying a thing. She was quiet for a moment and then asked for a price on all of it. My heart jumped and suddenly $5,000 came into my mind. As I held on to my latte with one hand, I wrote $5,000 on the papers she now held as the women in line kept interrupting, wanting to buy.

There is only one explanation as to where that number came from and why she left and quickly returned with the hotel manager and $5,000 cash in her hands: God. I had had less than fifty dollars left to my name and half a tank of gas. I knew I'd just experienced another sudden miracle, and I wanted to leap for joy right there in that hotel lobby. At the same time I wanted to fall to my knees and cry. I got into my car and drove to the far corner of the parking lot and cried tears of joy as I thanked my Abba. My God just kept providing for me. I was rested, I was pampered in that room, and He just sold everything I could imagine to a place I never knew existed. My God, how awesome are you!

I had a show in forty-eight hours and very little merchandise left. All that remained was a batch of scarves I'd left in the car and a collection of paintings. I made a few stops along the way in hopes of finding shoes and bags to paint. It was as if God called ahead and had a display waiting for me as I walked into Marshalls. On a table before me sat hot pink, lime green, and purple bags! The clearance section featured broken jewelry and ragtag items that I was purchasing to strip down to raw components. One more stop and I was supplied with all the bobbles and beads I needed to make more jewelry. The back of my car was like an artist's studio on wheels with paint, brushes, blank canvases, ribbon, lace, leather, and most anything needed to create. I quickly went to work and with the help of the Lord and a whole lot of coffee, I managed to recreate a full line for the show at Dennis's home.

I arrived at Dennis's with a car full of artsy fun for his show. Dennis and Jamie helped me set up. Excitement filled the air as Jamie and I created a retail gallery environment out of Dennis's home. Somehow the Lord had provided just what I needed to pack that place full of my art. Jamie and Dennis had a gorgeous display of appetizers, and Dennis greeted his guests with a beverage as they started pouring in.

I looked around and people stood in clusters talking and looking and totally engaged in my art. The rooms were filled with professionals and college professors. I was honored, happy, and humbled at the validation I felt again. Unworthiness seemed to vaporize that night and left no trace of its ugliness. Things were selling, and I was overcome with joy. Dennis called me over and introduced me to his friends Perry and Abe. They were extremely knowledgeable about art. They asked very technical questions about my work. Then Perry asked where I had earned my MFA. I stood there as if she had asked someone else and not me. I had zero education of any kind outside of cosmetology.

Dennis smiled and said, "Did you hear Perry? She wants to know where you received your MFA." My master of fine arts? Oh my goodness! I could feel myself blushing and told them that I didn't have an education, that God had just given me a creative spirit. They looked at me, stunned, and then looked at each other. Perry and Abe began to tell me about the art gallery they owned. Abe was an architect and worked in the loft of the exquisite gallery downtown close to the university hospital. Perry spoke first and asked if I would be interested in displaying at their gallery. Every piece that wasn't sold that evening to guests went to their gallery the next day! God had just opened another door, and I knew I was being kept in Iowa for a season and for His purpose. But I still didn't know where I would be or what that purpose was.

That night as I lay down to sleep in Dennis's guest room, I remembered a movie I'd seen about a field of dreams in Iowa. I knew God had fulfilled a field of dreams for me with provision to survive on. I decided to send most of what I had just made to repay the dental debt to my dad. I kept a little to survive on and had the promise of more to come from the gallery. That night, I slept like a baby again.

Pippy and I woke up in Dennis's guest room excited to attend the second phase of our classes together. We had met at the first phase. Pippy was a newfound friend and undiscovered cousin! That course was amazing and so were the people in it and facilitating it. I met Genny, a graduate student from Turkey, and formed an instant bond with her the first day. When we connected, we both knew it was for a lifetime. I was profoundly blessed by the weekend, but the joy came to an abrupt halt.

My attorney, Richard, called to let me know that I had to leave immediately. Damien was relentless. Just when I felt life might begin again, darkness reminded me that Damien wanted me dead and that he'd stalk me forever. I was told I had to appear in a Wisconsin court the next day. My new reality slapped me in the face. I left my new friends, promising to always keep in touch, and was halfway to Wisconsin and in a daze when my phone rang. It was Richard explaining that the court date had been manipulated by Damien again and was postponed. I stopped at a rest area on the interstate. I prayed prayers of worship and thankfulness. I'd experienced a weekend of profound blessings. There were financial blessings, and the people and

relationships that were forged were great gifts from Abba. I wondered if I had made the right decision to give most of what I'd made to Dad. In the excitement, I had mailed a check to him right away hoping I'd please him. Realistically, I didn't have much left. I asked God as I prayed to show me what to do. Should I continue on and return to Jo's in Wisconsin, or where was it that He was leading me?

As I prayed, Michael came to mind. Michael lived in Iowa. I love my brother Michael deeply. He had really been my only brother for many years. In my heart, I feared our kinship was mostly in my imagination. Michael seldom answered my calls or reached out to me since Mom had died. But the few times we did talk, he was his loving self. Michael was the only one of my brothers who would even talk to me since Mom's death. I've never known a harder worker or kinder human being than Michael. With God's nudge, I called him.

Without a second thought and with his arms wide open, Michael invited me to his home, which he shared with his girlfriend, Evelyn. There I found warmth and love. I learned how extremely loving Michael and Evelyn are to everyone around them, unconditionally and without any strings. I saw the two of them give and give in so many ways to their friends and their community.

I opened up to Michael about what was really going on in my life. I told him I'd been homeless for well over a year and could not find work. He asked me to stay in his guest room for as long as I needed. So there I was, in my little brother's home, knowing this was where God had led me.

I applied everywhere for work, hoping for a break. Everywhere I went I would see people rushing, hurrying to work, hurrying to school, and charging though life. I yearned to feel a part of anything again. It seemed like a lifetime ago that I had felt purpose or that I was of any value to anyone and wondered if I ever would be again. I tried to help Michael and Evelyn without butting into their worlds, and they seemed to be happy when I did. Dog walks, laundry, and keeping their place clean made me feel like I was earning some of my keep. When time allowed, I made more jewelry to send to the gallery.

That familiar desperate heartache of being a burden crept in. I knew that Michael's and Evelyn's kindness and generosity toward me took away so much privacy from them. That made me feel ashamed. Slowly, I began to sink into that dark place of depression again. As the months passed with no doors opening, I felt more ashamed and hopelessness crept back in. Darkness told me what a loser I was. I didn't fit in. When I'd walk into the grocery store, people would stare and look away if I smiled at them. That familiar and isolated feeling of misfit engulfed me.

I tried several local churches for Sunday services. I wanted to run out and just cry when I did. Even there, in the church, people stared at me. If I smiled, they turned quickly and walked the other way. I felt very out of place and judged in the two churches I visited. I tried to join a large international Bible study and was told it was full. They shrugged and told me to try next year. With that, I felt completely rejected and quit trying.

The money I had left was quickly dwindling as I sent promised payments to Dad and Richard, the lawyer. Every day, Dad asked if I had a job yet. That question deepened the hopelessness that was creeping back in. Daily, Richard pressured me for more money. He would threaten to "drop me if I didn't come up with more money" on a regular basis. I had grown to really dislike Richard and understand that I couldn't trust him. He was dishonest. That was like a punch in my stomach. However, I also knew I had paid him so much money and that I would have to start at square one with another lawyer. I just wanted the divorce over and done.

I was grateful for the gallery sales through Christmas, but after Valentine's Day, they dwindled. My bank account had fallen to below fifty dollars, and I found myself at the end of the rope again.

In a last ditch effort, I made a trip to the city I'd grown up in in Iowa to find work. My attempt was a dismal failure. I drove back unsuccessful, filled with deep sadness and rejection. I couldn't focus on driving and kept creeping off the road. I stopped at a dark, abandoned rest area on that highway. Suddenly, I found myself weeping to the point I could hardly breathe out of my damaged nose. I felt that familiar sense of darkness that had engulfed and surrounded me before. I wanted to die. I really did. I just couldn't bear to think of Julian living without his mom or hearing of my suicide. I also couldn't bear the shame I felt I brought to him. I felt despondent and finished. There was no fight left in my weary soul. I felt that God had given me help and I had let Him down too.

Over and over in my head, I heard what felt like tape recordings of Mom telling me to go to real college, not cosmetology school. I'd been on my own for almost a year when I'd decided to go to that school. In my youthful arrogance, I hadn't thought my parents had a right to any opinion of what kind of school I should attend if I was paying for all of it.

I thought about how I had worked so extremely hard in the hair styling competition arena and in developing my businesses over the years. I became the consummate overachiever. I'd been blessed with many years of worldly successes. But all of that meant nothing now. Nothing. My business experience was working against me. When I'd attempt to find any sort of work in the salon world, people were suspicious. They all wondered why I was there and what had happened to my business. When my résumé reflected the sales of my businesses, it was as if two and two were not adding up. Why would I need a job or be in the condition I was in after all the years of success?

The rejection ran very deep. The pressures on me were intense. I cried out to God to help me, and I laid my head on the steering wheel in that rest area parking lot. I thought maybe if I spent the night in the car I would just freeze. For the second time in my life, I felt God's physical presence. Strong, loving arms wrapped around me from behind. I sat up straight and almost felt His chin on my shoulder. He told me I would be okay. He reminded me that He doesn't lie. His word is truth. He is truth and light, and He had guided me here. He reminded me that He asked me to trust Him. I felt that peace again, and it engulfed me. I drove back to my brother's home, crawled into bed with my dog, and slept.

The next day my phone rang. It was Bobbie, a women I had met many years before when we were both young stylists on the competition circuit. She said she had heard that I was in town and asked what I was doing. I said I'd sold my salons and was not doing a thing. This was true, however, I omitted the little homeless part! She explained that she was a regional field manager for a privately held corporation that had eight colleges spanning three states. She asked if I would be open to meeting with her about a position at a college. I'd mentored many salon and spa professionals for years. I knew teaching would be a low-paying job, but I was excited. The meeting was set for the next morning, a Sunday, and the campus would be closed.

When we met, the huge, absolutely beautiful college campus I had just walked onto surprised me. I was also surprised to hear they needed me to be at the home office five hours away the next day to interview for the college administrator position! College administrator?! I had just spent the night before weeping and crying out to God and hating myself for not having any education and now I was being asked to interview for a position as the college administrator?! My God, my God! He was in this. The next day I left super early and ready to interview. They immediately offered me a huge salary with full benefits and gave me a key to the college. They said, "It's yours." They asked me to treat the school like it was my baby. They asked me to rehire and train a team of my own and to get the school on track for the successes I'd always had in business. The next chapter had begun. Overnight. Suddenly everything would change again. I'd truly experienced sudden miracle after miracle in Iowa.

Racism, Drugs, Gangs, and Jesus

Let us not become weary in doing good,
for at the proper time we will reap a harvest
if we do not give up.
Romans 12:12

I could hardly believe the opportunity before me. The school was large, beautiful, and state of the art. I toured the empty campus with Bobbie. At one time it had been a car dealership, but now it was a cosmetology, esthetics, massage therapy, and nail technology college, and the only college in the country accredited with an associate's program in health and beauty management. The classrooms were large and well equipped. The massive salon was modern and beautiful. The retail store had once been a huge glass showroom for cars. In addition to housing my office and the admissions department, it had a huge central front desk and a large retail store with gifts, cosmetics, and health and beauty supplies.

The spa had private and fully equipped rooms. A large bubbling water fountain separated classrooms and the computer labs from the guest service areas. Amongst all the bells and whistles, I immediately saw a lack of care and organization. The corporate office had disclosed that enrollment had drastically declined and that grade point averages were very low. No staff or students were there that day, but I sensed major internal problems. Sometimes all that sparkles isn't gold. I knew God had brought a huge challenge into my life. I was grateful and ready to dive in.

As I walked around campus that first day, I found that the classrooms were vacant. Off the student break room, the majority of students and my staff were hanging out on an outdoor patio. I opened the door to see all of them smoking cigarettes and marijuana. The majority of them jumped up and walked quickly back inside. However, a few students remained, glaring defiantly. When I asked them to leave the campus or return to the classroom, they grumbled racist comments and filed inside.

Only one remained. He was over six feet tall and had shoulders almost as broad. He sat glaring at me through his long, wild dreads. I asked him if he had heard me. He stood up with about six inches between us, hands on his hips, and asked me if I knew who he was and where he came from. I told him my concern was where he was going not where he had been. I told him he'd have the best I could give and the choice was his. He could live by my rules or leave, and if I saw drugs again the police would handle it. He stared me down. Inside, all five foot three of me was scared; but God gave me the courage to stand firmly. It seemed to be an eternal stare down. Then to my surprise, he turned, walked to the door, and politely held it open for me. Then he quietly returned to his classroom.

Quickly, I learned that the college was accepting newly released convicts from prison due to simple, fast funding. Most of these students had zero desire to be in school. They were there for the paycheck they received for attending. In the mix were members of a notorious violent gang. When they didn't show up for school, they were usually in jail. Some of them had violent criminal convictions. It didn't take long to see why enrollment was down and the local high school grads chose other colleges despite all the bells and whistles.

I was firm and loving to everyone, staff included. One day I had to suspend a woman for disruptive behavior in her classroom. When I did, she had freaked out in my office, flipping a glass table over before she raced out into the store. She threatened people, knocked down shelves, and called for family backup. I called 911. After her arrest and reports were filed, a police officer asked if he could have a private, off-the-record discussion with me. We went into my office.

He said the woman in the altercation was a family member of one of the most violent gang leaders in the area. He said to never have a word with her again, that I was putting my own life in danger. My God, my God! How had this happened? He suggested that we close the campus for the remainder of the day. The rest of the police stood outside my office. They told me to lock down the school and not allow anyone else in the building and to call 911 if anyone attempted.

I went to every classroom, calming those that remained. As I passed the student lounge, I spotted a friend of the girl who had just been taken away on her phone. This woman was holding the back door open! Outside a van pulled up and a bunch of young men hopped out and sprinted toward that door. When the woman saw me, she ran out and I locked it behind her. The police came, more reports were filed, and I sent everyone home for the remainder of the day.

While I spoke on the phone with corporate headquarters, I was walking the entire campus ensuring it was locked up. I had also assured the police I was leaving immediately. To my shock and dismay, none of this was a surprise to corporate. My heart sank, and I knew I had the challenge of my life in front of me or I would be faced with unemployment again. I noticed how the fear I'd been walking through in my own life had numbed me to the severity of what was happening on campus. Enouogh time had passed that there I was, after dark and after a day like this one had been, alone. I hung up; I could call the police again for an escort, or I could just go for it. I sprinted to my car, praying the whole way. My brother and Google immediately confirmed facts that had been laid out by the police. Michael knew the family name immediately. Evelyn just stared at me in disbelief.

Music has always talked to me, and that night a song played over and over in my mind . . . *Greater things are yet to come, greater things are still to be done in this city* . . . God told me to trust Him. He always had been and still was my protector and my provider.

Each faculty member and every student were required to meet in a large theory room for morning roll call. I attended the roll call every morning. I read to them from a daily Christian devotional. It was the same devotional I used to read in the park by Dad's house. It had brought me through some very hard times, and I prayed it might impact them too. They were surprised and whispered to each other as I read. Gradually, they started trickling into my office. One by one they came. Students and staff confided to me that the Scriptures had touched them. They told me they felt the words were written just for them, like God was speaking directly to them. I shared many special moments with students and staff. I knew that God was at work in them. They were healing from many unfair circumstances in their worlds and getting an education and a career in the process. I was finding a purpose and deep healing as I helped others.

I felt like law enforcement as the students continued to challenge me every chance they could and to break the rules. One day I closed the campus and took the entire student body out to the parking lot. We tie dyed shirts and had a crazy fun time. Slowly, I was earning their respect and the campus was growing. Corporate informed me that I wasn't allowed to share my religious beliefs with the students or staff. I continued doing it anyway, and the students loved it. Soon there was happiness on the campus, revenues were growing quickly, GPAs were up, and students were winning awards. Corporate stopped bothering me about sharing my "religious" beliefs.

The man who had challenged me outside during my first few days on campus graduated and opened his own business. His massive shoulders house a massive heart. He is a really good man and a great daddy to his girls. He became like my own bodyguard. That man stood up for me, and no one messed with me. I will never forget him. He is so very special to me. All he needed was to be loved and pushed to be his best. He needed someone to believe in him. I spent a year on that campus with much blood, sweat, and tears. The staff and students have impacted my life forever. It brings me great joy to still hear from them and know I made a difference in their lives.

I spent long hours at school, and the rest of my time I was mostly alone as God worked deeply inside of me. The loneliness was horrible. I very seldom heard from Michael and Evelyn after I left their home. I always wondered why.

The constant fear was palpable in my little apartment. Damien had found me quickly on the campus and knew where I lived. I clutched on to that order of protection. It was broken enough times that I was told he'd be jailed on the next attempt. Despite all the fear, I learned a lot that year. God held my hand and breathed life back into me tiny baby steps at a time.

Simple things brought me huge joy. For the first time in more than twenty-two months, I had my own bedroom and bathroom. I cooked in my own kitchen and had a couch to just be. I will never take a home for granted again. My order of protection was extended, and the judge firmly told me I needed to change my name and my birth certificate.

To my surprise, the name change was healing. Not hearing at all from two of my three brothers through homelessness and severe trauma had made me realize that I didn't have a biological family and carrying that old name had been painful. The name "Ada Madison," which is not my birth name, represented new life to me. It was a surreal moment to be handed a new birth certificate. Everyone in that courtroom stared at me in pity. I had grown so used to running, the constant fear numbing my emotions. When the judge strongly recommended a complete change including my Social Security number, it sunk in for the first time. I let it melt away from my memory when Judge Miller said the same thing. This was not a dream that I would wake up from. This was real, and my life would never, ever be the same. As my first year at the college was drawing to an end, I sensed that soon God would be taking me to the unknown again.

Small Step, Giant Leap

When I am afraid I put my trust in You.
Psalm 56:3

Iowa was a time of deep healing for me. While guiding and inspiring students, I found a piece of self-worth. I was grateful for the financial provision. It was divine and designed to bring healing. Although my income was great, the financial demands were greater. Damien dragged the legal process out as long as he could. I discovered that he had been day trading my money online and lost everything I had ever had. Any hopes of uncovering hidden funds evaporated as the reports came in.

Julian was in and out of college and directionless. One day he announced he was moving to Seattle to attend school. My heart stopped, and I prayed he would change his mind. I was happy he had the courage to reach for his dreams, but my heart broke as he left my home that last time. I remembered leaving Iowa when I was his age. I prayed God would put angels along his path to protect him just as He has done for me. I prayed Julian would forgive me. I had always tried to be his rock. I felt more like sand than a rock now. As my faith deepened, Julian was angry with little to no faith left. I knew I couldn't fix it and that I only had one choice, to put my faith in Abba. I had to trust God. Julian is the greatest gift God has ever given me. God knew him first, and His word teaches that He actually loves Julian more than

I do. I couldn't imagine a love greater than my love for Julian. God gave me peace, and the anxiety I felt lessened but the painful sorrow of Julian's move remained.

I learned to know God's voice during that time in Iowa. I learned to lean on Him and know I could trust Him. The world had shown me I couldn't trust people. He'd shown me that He will never leave me or forsake me. It was His promise to me, and I knew that God couldn't lie. I held on to those promises. I experienced many nights of primal fear as Damien continued to stalk and threaten me. I was tired of police reports and fear. I clung to God and nightly calls with Gee.

Through all this time, Gee had continued to call me almost every day. She was a lifeline to the world. Most days, the only conversations I had outside of the ones with my students or staff were on the phone with Gee and Dad. I trusted Gee and talked to her about everything. She always seemed to know when another crushing blow would come in advance and call me to warn or console me. She prayed me out of many panicky moments when I thought I might be killed. She knew every single intimate detail of my life. It seemed odd to remember that it'd been twelve years since we had seen each other. We'd grown very close over the phone.

During that year at the college, my divorce was finalized, my name was changed, and a new birth certificate was issued. Most importantly,

I came out of twenty-two months of homelessness. As my first-year anniversary at the college neared, I sensed change was coming again. In my heart I knew God was going to move me again. I just didn't know how or where.

I had two weeks of paid vacation and decided to visit Gee in Florida. The thought of seeing each other was exciting to both of us. I told Gee I felt God was going to move me again. She concurred that she'd felt the same and encouraged me to consider Florida. Before I left, I took advantage of the health insurance I had for the first time in a long time and had all my "annual" checkups, which included a mammogram.

When I arrived in Florida, Gee was waiting at the gate. She looked different than I remembered, but then twelve years had passed since we'd last seen each other. I had a very strange feeling in my stomach, and my heart felt uneasy when I looked into her eyes. The soft, motherly voice I'd come to love did not match up with Gee's eyes. I could see she felt uneasy when she saw me too. I now know that she saw the light of Jesus in me, and it made her uncomfortable. I also now know she's not a follower of Jesus and dabbles in the occult. I've learned you don't dabble with the devil. To dabble in the occult is like adding a small dollop of arsenic to a glass of water. Poison is poison, and a dab of the devil can kill you.

On the surface we had a good time together, but inside I felt a strange conflict. A few days before my planned return, I received a call from my doctor in Iowa. The voice on the other end told me the mammogram showed that I needed to get to the hospital for a biopsy immediately. I explained that I was on vacation. The voice said that I shouldn't wait. There was that fear again. They scheduled a biopsy for me in Florida the next morning. Gee drove me to the appointment. Inside I thought, *Yeah, cancer. I probably have cancer now, and I will die the way Mom did. It's probably all been caused by stress.*

After the biopsy and waiting an hour and a half in the lobby, I was ready to hear a breast cancer diagnosis. A nurse appeared and seemed surprised to see me sitting there. They were closing the office and had forgotten me. I was truly surprised when the doctor informed me of my test results: benign. But the test had delayed my travels back to the security of my job. As I had sat in that lobby waiting to be told I had cancer, I'd felt God pressuring me to make arrangements to move to Florida. I was afraid to leave my income. I was afraid to not have a single soul I knew around me again. Gee was not who I thought she was, and I wasn't sure why God was leading me to Florida. I wanted to just get home and take my time deciding. I was wrestling with God. I did not want to leave what I saw as my security at work.

On what I thought was my last day in Florida, I visited an old colleague of mine. I pulled up alongside his business's all-glass building and saw his name displayed on a side door. I stepped toward the welcome mat. It was a false entrance with very deep, tiny gravel rocks that had just been poured. I was wearing high platform sandals and went head over heels crashing into the glass door. My foot broke. In a flash I remembered falling and breaking my hand before and how it felt like I had been pushed. This moment felt eerily the same. It was surreal and had happened in slow motion. The sound of my foot breaking and my pain made me instantly dizzy and nauseous. As I sat in the emergency room with a bandaged breast from the biopsy and a freshly wrapped up foot, I felt cursed. I kept asking God why? Why did these things keep happening to me?

Now there was no possible way for me to leave Florida and maneuver an airport and parking lot alone. I had driven myself to the airport and left my car parked in the long-term lot. I had no one to call for help, and I lived up a flight of stairs. My condo was the safest place I could find, but it also had multiple staircases that I would have to maneuver. I could hardly believe what had just happened. There I was in a whole lot of pain, wanting to go home and unable to.

Then, suddenly, a huge tropical depression came through and poured rain every single day and even shut down most flights! Since I was stuck in Florida, I went to the beach anyway and sat under an umbrella alone and with a hugely swollen foot and bandaged breast. I felt like Chicken Little. I was having my own little pity party. This was not how I had planned my vacation and surely not the way I might have dreamed about extending it. Then, suddenly, God spoke to me extremely clearly. It was almost audible. He told me I was staying and to find a place to live. I asked Him about Gee but He didn't answer.

My phone rang and interrupted my conversation with God. It was the federal government investigative office telling me I needed to get to the closest Social Security office within twenty-four hours. They had been researching my case for a year to determine whether to issue me a full new identity with a new Social Security number. I was somewhat accustomed to their calls, but they'd never been urgent. I started to explain my physical challenges and why I was going to be delayed getting back to Iowa when they interrupted me saying, "NO." They told me it was imperative that I go to a local Social Security office and to "go right away, today if possible." Their urgency worried me. I drove myself to the local Social Security office and hobbled in soaking wet. They gave me a number and told me to be seated.

When they called my number, every person who worked in that office came forward or peeked over files or from around corners. They had me show photo identification and proceeded to give me paperwork that stated officially, as of that minute, with my signature on June 26, 2012, that I had started a new life, as a new person, with a new Social Security number. The man helping me said he had been there for twenty-five years and had never seen this before. He asked me what had happened. All I told him was that I had a very violent ex. He said, "God Bless you, and I pray your new start brings you great joy." God had just confirmed through the Social Security officer that I was beginning my next season in a new location again.

God's joy filled me, and I smiled as I left and obeyed Him immediately. I drove around and found a cute tiny house in an affordable area and rented it on the spot. I'm not sure how I did it but I flew home, packed myself, painted a mural in Michael's new kitchen, and ten days later, was on the road with my nephew James driving a moving truck. With a broken foot, I was following behind him in my car. I was excited about another new beginning and trusting God for my new life. I'd secured a position at a salon before I left and had enough money to survive for a few months. I also had a very large income tax refund on the way. I would be financially secure for six months. This would give me plenty of time to develop a business again.

As I followed James across the country, we would stop every few hours to fill up. I would get gas for both vehicles and more junk food for him. We stopped for the night somewhere in the mountains of Tennessee. It was a rural area, but we found a decent looking hotel online that allowed my pooch, Rosie, and also the moving truck. We rolled in almost on empty as we stopped for gas before we checked in for the night. My debit card held all the money I had. James scanned it to pump, and I took his list inside to get his junk food. At the checkout, a turban-clad guy who didn't speak clear English said my card didn't work. I stepped outside, and James said it had been declined at the pump as well. I assumed it was because of the massive gas purchases over multiple states, and I called the number on the back of the card. After an hour on the phone, I learned that the IRS had levied my bank account and that every single cent I once had had been taken. I had no idea why. I was expecting a large return from the IRS. Suddenly, in the middle of the night, I felt an all-to-familiar financial and safety panic moment. There we were, James and I, with no gas in the huge moving truck, hungry and tired, in the middle of the night and in unfamiliar territory with no money.

I did the only thing I knew to do. I prayed and called my dad. God began blessing me through Dad that night. The man at the checkout took a verbal credit card number from me for a card that did not have my name on it, over the phone, in the middle of the night, for more than $150 in gas. It happened again for food. It happened again for our hotel. And it happened again in Florida for more gas and more food. In today's world that's impossible, but it happened. It happened over and over as we drove to Florida. Sudden worry followed by sudden miracles— again. I knew if I could just get to Florida, I could fix whatever mistake had happened with the IRS.

On Monday morning, I called the IRS right away and made an appointment for that afternoon. The IRS agent had paperwork with my signature on it. It quickly became clear that about a year into my marriage to Damien, unbeknownst to me, I had signed paperwork assuming all liability for massive tax debt he had from over a decade before I ever even met him. Damien had handled all of our taxes and accounting, and I had blindly signed on the line he asked me to. I learned there was absolutely nothing I could do to reverse the levy. I learned they had also intercepted the large refund I was expecting. I was shocked and speechless. I broke down in tears and began telling the IRS agent my story. He told me they would "relieve" me of any further responsibility beyond the levy and refund interception that had already been irrevocably seized. I also learned he owed massive amounts of money to the IRS.

Legal advice confirmed what the IRS officer had told me: There is no way to get money back from the IRS after it has been levied. I was told that to recuperate the money unfairly taken from me, I would have to sue Damien. There was absolutely no possible way I could begin to think I would sue Damien and ever feel safe again. And for that matter, if I did, would I recover a dime anyway? Damien had now successfully stolen every single penny I had ever worked for past, present, and even future. He had even managed to steal money that I had earned at the college long after I had left him and after our divorce was final. As I sat there trying to comprehend what had just happened, I had a memory of Damien stealing future child support money from my son and me. He had truly squeezed every single dime—past, present, and future—from Julian and me.

A few days later, Gee emailed me to say, "Your God has gotten you this far, and He will see you through." She went on to say, "You'll be fine, but I am on a different path. God will answer your prayers. Goodbye." On that same day, I was falsely accused of stealing, publicly shouted at, and fired from the new salon job I'd secured. I had a home, but I felt homeless again. I also felt very, very alone. I wondered why I had left the security of work and a tightly secured upstairs condo. I was now in a sketchy neighborhood with zero security in a city where I knew no one. My other two brothers and their families lived close by but refused every attempt I made to contact them. It was a painful, final realization that they hated me and wanted no association with me. I felt like I was in outer space, floating and unable to breathe. I could see the spacecraft that held others and provided life, but my lifeline was cut. I was on the outside looking in to others with life. I couldn't breathe and was floating away into dark nothingness again, completely alone.

I had no choice but to fully lean on God and not on my own understanding because absolutely nothing in the world made sense. I encouraged myself with the reminder that eventually it would make sense. I loved God with all my heart, but my heart was broken into many pieces. I was drowning in rejection, abandonment, unworthiness, shame, and a sense of profound loss and failure. Without Jesus, there is absolutely no way I could have survived.

Breaking through to the Prophetic Voice of God

I will instruct you and teach you in the way you should go;
I will counsel you with my loving eye on you.

The physical wounds were healing, but the intense emotional trauma lingered. The joy of renting that cute little house close to the beach faded as the nights grew longer and darker. A vacant lot next door with a For Sale sign showed barely above the thick overgrown weeds that filled it. I hated that lot and the fear it inspired in me. My mind told me that anyone or anything could be completely hidden in it. From my bed, I'd look out my window into that lot at night and imagine snakes and Damien, and I'd fill up with sleep-depriving fear. It felt like a dark cloud had followed me to Florida. I felt like I was cursed. I couldn't believe I'd been fired from the salon job and accused of things that never could have happened. It hurt me deeply and left me emotionally debilitated.

I very quickly learned that the few people I had connected with in Florida were only after what they thought I had to offer them. When they realized I did not have the financial resources they had assumed I had, they grew distant. The emotional trauma deepened as people stepped away. Two married couples I had met in a church and that I looked up to as honest Christians suddenly and abruptly walked away from me. They accused me of horrible, untrue things. I felt discarded, rejected, abandoned, and completely alone again. I found myself asking God why. Why was I being accused of things that had never happened? Why had He led me to Florida when I only found deep rejection here again? I had been stripped of any sense of financial security I'd thought I had when Damien and the IRS had taken my meager savings and tax refund. My hope in family was futile. My plans to develop a new business began with terrible, untrue accusations and public humiliation. Then came a blow I could have never been prepared for. This time I was falsely accused, rejected, and abandoned by the body of Christ. I felt like I'd been robbed of my heart and affections again. I loved these people, and I trusted them. They had taken everything I had of value with the promise of their teenage daughter selling it on eBay for a commission. They also "borrowed" valuables to display in their homes that I had stored through all my homelessness. Now the very few valuable things I had left and held dear to my heart, even my grandmother's keepsakes, were in their possession as they walked out of my life. I was never paid or saw any of it again. These couples had letters like MD behind their name, served on the board of the church and preached from the pulpits. I trusted them. They absconded with more than all my valuables, they stripped me of any ounce of trust I had left in people.

I truly didn't know how I was going to make it. I was alone, afraid, and thought I was defeated. I left the little house and downsized to a very small shared space, but it still was not enough. I had to start liquidating everything I had to survive. Within a few months, I had liquidated to the point of no furniture. In the process, I survived on the same thing that had carried me through almost two years of homelessness. I did hair in kitchens and sold art anywhere I could. I visited church after church and found a social climbers club or a bunch of judgment and religion. Sadness blanketed me. I had a hard time imagining ever climbing out of the darkness that seemed to continue to stalk me.

I'd been in many churches, in many states. I'd been in Bible studies and support groups and shelters and Christian crisis centers. Now my new friends, who I loved and confided in *and* shared intimate details of my pain and story, had hurt me deeply when they took from me the very few things I had left to my name. I had felt safe and trusted them because they were church elders and leaders. I've had many believers on my path. They all shared the desire to know details of my life like a scary movie entices the thrill-seeker. It used to amaze me how people seemed to enjoy hearing of my pain. It deepened my feeling of being a misfit and that I would never find home, a place to fit in. They also shared something else in common: Not one single "Christian" person had ever offered to pray for me. Not since that day I met Jesus when Pastor Tim had offered to pray for me had one single person prayed for me. Except Gee. And as Gee had told me, she didn't follow "my God."

One day, I visited a home group and I was prayed over for the first time in my life. I quickly dissolved into silent tears that I didn't know I had left. I was a private person, and very few times in my life had I cried in front of anyone. I cried years of pent-up, held back tears, silently. God spoke through the home group. They were saying things I'd never even heard before. In their prayers they began "binding and calling out spirits" of physical, sexual, and emotional abuse, abandonment, rejection, and so much more. They told me to renounce things and they were taking authority over spirits that had taunted me my entire life. I felt things melting off of me as I obediently followed their direction knowing that God was healing me. Very deep hurts and wounds that had been in me since I was a little girl were exposed in the living room as complete strangers surrounded me. Nothing was left uncovered. God exposed it all. Suddenly, I felt lighter. The heaviness, oppression, and depression had lifted. Later, I learned that I had experienced deliverance.

The only thing I ever knew about deliverance was that Burt Reynolds had starred in a movie of the same name many years ago. I didn't understand spiritual warfare or what those words even meant. I didn't even know the devil was real. But I did know that the heaviness was leaving for the first time since my world had crashed. The Lord began teaching me so much. My relationship with Jesus grew in my extreme brokenness. I began to really hear Him every day. I learned what it meant to live completely by spirit. God had been leading me for two years, but now I learned how to tune into Him for my every single move. I spoke with Him twenty-four/seven. My spiritual eyes were opening to so very much. Quickly, I realized I was seeing things that not everyone saw. I saw goodness in people everywhere. I also saw their hearts. I could see what was hurting them.

I found a place to live in a safe area where I could work from home. Suddenly, there I was again, sleeping on a floor and surrounded by art and art supplies. I had a very small amount of cash, which I used to purchase salon equipment and supplies rather than a bed. I opened my own little salon in my kitchen. It's funny how people didn't seem to notice my extreme poverty. Many weeks, I could barely afford food. But somehow God just kept providing what I needed to go another day.

God took all He had taught me and put it into action with on-the-job ministry training in that tiny kitchen salon. He was training me to minister His Love, the same love He'd poured into me. I learned to hear His voice tell what people needed and to pray into it. I witnessed many profound miracles in that little kitchen salon. People would stream in thinking they were there for hair. God would show me what they needed sometimes before they even got in the door. It brought me great joy thinking that people had come for a color and a cut, but instead had found God.

I often joked that my haircuts started with an art consultation, followed by prayer, and then baptism in the shampoo bowl! I prayed for many, many people in that little kitchen salon. It was a very unique ministry and truly God's training ground for me. It was a far cry from the huge salons and glamour of my past, but I loved it. People received more than beauty; they received healing and beauty not just on the outside but deep inside of their hearts too.

I was barely making it financially. I did a lot of hair free for abused women or people I could see were in great need. God provided my every single need, and I ministered His love. As I look back on all the provision He has gifted me, it blows me away. He always provided exactly what I needed at the exact right time.

Once, after a haircut, someone left me a little note with $500 in it. Another $500 check and a very kind note was handed to me after I visited a prayer group one night. A young man had come to my door to tell me God had told him to give me a gift. When he left, I saw a $2,000 check on my counter. Without it, I would have not been able to make it that month. Every gift was exactly what I needed to survive. No more, no less. Twice, I was tipped $1,000 for haircuts.

People also showed up with groceries and things I needed at the exact right moment. One day, a young man from the local pool broke down in tears with me. He was struggling financially, and his girlfriend had left him. He confided in me that he didn't even have food. I had twenty dollars allocated for food for myself that week, but I still had some things left in my cupboard. I went to the store and bought him all the things Julian loved. Somehow the Lord grew the value of the twenty dollars as I shopped. It looked like far more.

I delivered the bags of groceries to the young man. He was busy teaching a swim lesson to children, so I quietly left them in his office. He called me later and in tears. I told Him those groceries were from Jesus. They were. When I got home, one of my clients stopped over unannounced with a bag of groceries for me and a $200 gift card for more. My neighbor would pop over with chocolate or homemade goodies fresh out of her oven all the time.

One day, I heard the Lord tell me to go to the store and buy "real food" for myself. I had been buying only what was cheapest that week at the store. I never really cooked for myself. He said go buy ingredients and cook. I went to the store and began putting in my cart fresh ingredients, spices, and things I hadn't purchased in a very long time. I was feeling like I shouldn't be spending rent money as I was waiting in the checkout line. Then, suddenly, I was told that my entire cart had just been paid for. I was blown away. I was surviving on below-poverty-level income. My heavenly Father was caring for me.

After many months of no furniture I began searching on Craigslist for cheap furniture and found a table and chairs in my neighborhood.

Buying these would allow me to have Bible studies in my home and create art at a table. There was also this yellow, beat-up old leather loveseat and ottoman. The set looked like a cat-scratching post. The owners practically offered to give it to me. The Lord encouraged me to get it and to paint it like I had always done with my shoes. I remember saying to myself that I couldn't paint a couch! God asked me why. I thought, *Yeah, why not?* I do a permanent process on leather, and I thought it might be kind of cool. So I came home with the loveseat too.

I went to work on the table first. I sanded it down and painted it and the chairs. Each chair was uniquely different from the next. The results were wild and funky, Ada style. It needed a little something, and God brought to my memory

a torched resin process I had used to create tiny pieces of jewelry. I decided to try it on this huge table. The results were fabulous!

Then I went to work on the couch. I cleaned it up, stripped it down, and began hand painting designs into it. Soon the dingy cat scratch couch was popping with bright tulips and foiled blades of stylized grass. It turned out pretty darned cool. Everyone loved it, and my house started to make me feel like I was going to really live again. It was alive, bright, joyous, and I felt God with me. That old couch became like a prayer closet to me. It's saturated in tears, prayer and worship. I've prayed for many people sitting on that couch and witnessed Gods miraculous healing hand on many battered souls nestled in that old yellow couch.

I had slept on the floor for six months when I woke up to a birthday call from Dad. He said, "This is your Father speaking." This was not his normal talk. I knew it was God talking to me through Dad. He said, "Write this credit card number down and go buy a bed and a couch. Buy a dresser too. And don't buy crap, Ada. Get good stuff because this is from your father." Suddenly, I was no longer sleeping on a floor at night. I had a bed and what would soon become another canvas, a gray leather couch.

One day a woman I had never met came to my home for Bible study. Her name was Ann and she was full of light and joy. When everyone had left and I was cleaning up I found a check for $1000 under Ann's napkin. It was exactly what I needed in order to pay my bills that month. As I gave of myself to others, God found ways to bless me. Ann and I have become close friends. God not only helped me financially through Ann, He brought a wonderful friend into my life.

I kept ministering in my kitchen salon and God kept providing for me in intimate and amazing ways. One day I was chatting with a lady who was getting a long and involved hair color done. We were discussing flowers. She was dating an extravagant man who sent her flowers all the time. She asked me why I never dated. I explained that I had messed up that part of my life by relying on my own choices. I told her that I knew God created everything in the universe and surely I trusted Him to bring my husband to me. I told her that God was the only one in my life and that I was sure when He was done with me He would bring my husband. I told her that until then, God is my date. I think she thought I was nuts.

This woman told me that she hated seeing me all alone in that condo and that I deserved to be courted and sent flowers. Over the course of the next hour, and in her presence, I had not one, not two, but three bouquets of flowers delivered to me and a potted orchid from four people! There is no way to even make this stuff up. They were thank yous from clients and people I had been ministering to that I never could've expected. Abba was providing for me intimately and so lovingly. It ministered to my client's heart. She was as touched, tearful, and amazed as I was.

One day I awoke sensing God's nudge to donate every single piece of clothing that I didn't wear. I was clinging on to clothes that were the old me. I had a very small wardrobe and seventy-five empty hangers when I was done. I took the pieces to a Christian Outreach donation center where no money is ever exchanged. Everything they receive is given away freely to those in need. Twenty-four hours later a person I

had never met included me in a backstage, behind-the-scenes shopping spree at Chico's Design Lab. One-of-a-kind pieces were one to three dollars each. I'd been given a $100 tip that morning for a haircut, and I knew it was Him. I took my $100 to the shopping spree in childlike anticipation. When I brought these bags of clothes home, I was so full of joy! They were bright, fun, creative, and filled—you guessed it— with exactly seventy-five hangers.

I hosted a prayer group at my house one weekend and a new guest came. She was enthralled with all of my art. She took pictures and asked a lot of questions before and after our worship time. I later learned she is a published author and freelance writer for an affluent magazine in South Florida. She called me a few weeks later with news. She had submitted the photos she had taken, and I was selected for the Feature Article and voted the Rising Design Star! The magazine published an amazing article about my art and made a film about my work. This was God blessing the work of my hands.

When the used car I had purchased broke down beyond repair, I had traded it in on a very inexpensive lease. That lease was coming to an end. When I had leased it three years earlier, I thought that surely I would be able to purchase a car in a few years. But I was surviving because God provided, not because I had any money in the bank or credit established to purchase a car. I did the only thing I knew how to do. I took it to God. I asked Him to help me. I noticed that I lived close to a bus line. I felt grateful for the time I had a car and decided that if I was to be without a car again, I was okay with it. He would help me find a way to get the things I needed. Suddenly, God provided a 1998 Mercedes SLK convertible for me with less than 20,000 miles. The mechanic said it was the most pristine car he'd ever seen. There were still stickers on the motor. God told me to paint the interior leather of the car.

At the same exact time, a new and dear friend from the pool came to me one day and quietly handed me an envelope with a $5,000 check in it as we left our class at the pool. She said, "I don't need it and don't care if you ever pay me back." She asked me to please invest in what I needed to paint more and to start building a collection of furniture. What blessed me the most was her belief in me. God said He would make sure I could pay her back. I knew then that He was in it; she was another gift from Him. God told me to trust Him. He said He had a place for every piece I would create and would provide a way for me to pay her back with great joy. I asked Him why people just kept giving to me. I had never, ever asked for a dime or let on to anyone that I was in need. No one had any idea of how desperate my financial situation was. But He did. He was teaching me to trust Him and to lean on Him and only Him. When He gives, there is no sorrow added.

In a few short months, my home was bursting with unspeakable joy. My friend went with me, and we found fantastic Italian leather pieces of furniture. I decided I would use them to begin building a portfolio.

While I was working on the new pieces, I was also working on my car's interior.

Suddenly, I felt a spiritual sort of shift in the air. I sensed change again. The art editor of the city's newspaper contacted me. They wanted to do a feature article on my collection. My God how He provides! They interviewed me and were blown away. Then I showed them my car. They filmed my car and told me they were launching a new high-end magazine catering to the affluent of South Florida. I was in their launch issue with a centerfold spread with my cute little car interior and lots of hand-painted leather furniture. They published not one but two articles in the newspaper. Those articles trended as number one online, and they made a videography of our interview as well. Several other local papers followed suit. Only God.

Soon afterward, I received a call from the most prestigious museum in the city. They wanted to come and see my art. They told me they were considering me for their studio tour. God blessed me by bringing hundreds and hundreds of people right through my home studio! In a few short months, He brought me from sleeping on a hard tile floor in a depressed environment to a bright, happy, and joy-filled home. I often tell people my walls are saturated in prayer, worship, and deep, deep healing. He has told me He's with me and will provide for my every need. God asked me to step away again from the security and the intense work the salon had become. He told me to trust Him. I did as I prepared for the huge museum show.

During this period of intense creative release, the Lord began speaking many things to me. I always have praise music on, and I worship and pray as I create. I am in constant communion with Him. But He began speaking to me in dreams and visions more than ever before. A vivid and very real dream awakened me one morning. I could feel the coolness of the day and smell the flowers that surrounded me. It seemed very real. In this vision, I was a bride. I was in a huge church filled with white flowers. It was ornately painted with a balcony and angels on the ceilings with golden detailed plaster moldings. I later learned it was Times Square Church in New York City. I was standing at the back and realized I was the bride and I was getting married at that moment. I suddenly realized that I had a short wedding dress on and it was strapless. I felt very self-conscious and couldn't figure out why I had a dress on like this. It was beautiful, but not for me.

Then the music started, and I was supposed to begin walking down the aisle. I reluctantly took a step forward and felt a pull on the dress. I looked behind me and the fluffy white train that flowed from my dress was about a city-block long. I was afraid that if I walked, the weight of that train would pull my dress down. I was self-conscious and ready to cry. A man's hand came under my chin and lifted my face up to his. It was Him. It was Jesus. He told me I was His bride. He told me He was very proud of me exactly as I was. He told me I was beautiful and that He would never leave me or forsake me. I had flowers in my arms, and I threw them into the air as I jumped up and wrapped my arms around His neck, hugging Him tightly.

God was healing my self-rejection and self-hatred. He reminded me that He lived in me and I was rejecting Him when I was so unkind to myself. Like many women, I only saw glaring imperfections. Like many women, the tapes of abusive moments in my life played over and over in my mind. He told me I was His masterpiece and He adored me just exactly as I was.

One night while I was worshipping, I received a strong and clear vision from the Lord. He told me exactly the painting He wanted me to create. He showed me every detail. I came home that night and could hardly sleep as I was creating that piece over and over in my mind. Over the next week, a triptych painting spanning twelve feet wide began to emerge.

It is a huge crystal-capped wave and is titled *Living Waters*.

It was four months later that *Living Waters* was featured in the magazine editorial. Several weeks later, someone pointed out to me, the bride. That painting held within it the vision the Lord had given me of Times Square Church, my wedding, and Jesus. As I looked at the magazine, all I could see was the bride within! She is on the right in her short dress tossing her flowers into the air with abandon. And the train, the long, long train, extends the length of the painting as the sparkling crest of the wave. This piece hangs in my living room, and now I can't look at it without seeing the bride. My God, how awesome are You! He was speaking and confirming. I began asking Him to show me more of His heavenly images.

Prophetic paintings began to flow and so did words He gave me while

I painted with Him. *Warrior* came to me next. This painting is large, four feet by five feet. She was made strong in His image but had a tender heart filled with His empathy and compassion. She is His bride, spotless and pure. She awaits for Him to direct her every move. I saw her with combat boots sitting in a field of abstract flowers or art. She was abiding under the shadow of His wing. He began not only showing me what to paint but giving me a prophetic message to share.

I received this message as I painted her. Warrior . . . You are not alone My bride, you are not alone. What the world tried to bury My resurrection power has burst forth. You are the apple of My eye, and I will always keep you safely tucked under the shadow of my wings. You are beautifully and wonderfully made in My image by Me. I make no mistakes. You have been delivered from all fear and made whole for such a time as this. Go forth. I am making beauty from ashes. You will lead many to freedom and truth. You are My warrior and My precious bride. I love you.

Zechariah 4:6: Not by might, not by power but by My spirit.

Psalm 17:8: Keep me as the apple of your eye; hide me in the shadow of your wings.

Psalm 91:4: He will cover you with his feathers, and under his wings you will find refuge; his faithfulness will be your shield and rampart.

Psalm 34:7-9: The angel the Lord shall encamp around those who fear Him and deliver them.

Esther 4:14: Yet who knows whether you have come to the kingdom for such a time as this?

I had barely completed *Warrior* when He gave me another image. This time it was another huge painting of His bride under the open floodgates of heaven. He showed me a vision and exactly what the colors should be. He guided my every stroke. He spoke these words to me as I painted "His bride":

Do not grow weary, precious one, for I have been with you every step of the way. I have watched as you have selflessly become My hands, My feet, and have spoken from My heart the words I put upon your

lips. You see, when you stumbled and fell, I was there. You were never alone. My angels have collected every tear you have ever cried and kept them in a bottle. You are the apple of my eye! I have prepared a feast for you, My bride, in the presence of your enemies. The time is now! Come forth! I am walking you on water as you step into your purpose, destiny, and calling in Me. Come, the floodgates of heaven are opening . . .

Psalm 17:8: Keep me as the apple of the eye; Hide me in the shadow of Your wings.

Psalm 56:8: I keep track of all my sorrows. I have collected all my tears in your bottle. I have recorded each one in your book.

Psalm 20:4: May He grant you according to your heart's, fulfill all your purpose.

Psalm 23:5: You prepare a table before me in the presence of my enemies. You anoint my head with oil; my cup overflows.

This body of work keeps growing. The most profound experience I have had so far painting with Jesus is creating a painting of Him. He told me I was going to paint His face. I didn't want to. I had never "seen" what He looks like, only faint moments of seeing His eyes. I've never liked any other artist's interpretation of Him. He revealed many things to me over the course of a few weeks and why it was important for me to create this painting. I've never felt nervous painting, but I truly didn't know what to do or where to begin on this painting of Jesus. I had always started a painting by doing background and large areas, layering and getting more and more detailed as I went. This time He said no. He told me to paint His eyes first, and He told me that He would show me what to do. I paint large scale, and suddenly I had a huge canvas with only very real looking kind, sensitive, and loving eyes staring at me. They are blue and green and brown and gray and dark, almost black. I started to cry as I looked at them. I began to see what He was showing me. I sang, worshipped, and danced around with that paintbrush until He was done. I have never in my life experienced such heavenly joy creating. When I was finished, He gave me this message:

Come to Me. Come to me. I will heal your broken body. I will heal your broken heart. I will soothe your burdened soul. What the world discards as trash, I see as diamonds! You are my child, and I am your Abba. That is right, I am

your Father! I knit you together in your mother's womb. You are not a mistake. You have a purpose and a destiny that only I can reveal to you. You are the apple of my eye. I see all your hurts, all the rejection you have endured, and the emotional scars that linger. I cry with you.

My angels have collected every single tear you have ever cried and keep them in a bottle. If you will just take my hand and walk with me, I will carry you through every trial this world throws at you. Together we will celebrate true love! You were not meant to be alone or abused. No! Trust me. I have your perfect partner for your journey. I will bring you patience and perseverance. You will walk with joy! All your life will be filled with a peace that surpasses all understanding. When you humble yourself and take my hand, your meekness will bring deliverance and healing. You will find that goodness and kindness abound. Take my hand, precious one. I will guide you. And one day I will tell you, "Well done," and together we will step into eternity. I love you.

As this body of work continues to grow, I have no idea where God is leading me. I can only trust Him and continue to put one foot in front of the other. Still, there are moments that Satan tries to taunt me. He tells me I will be homeless again. He reminds me of my biological family and how they all hate me and have abandoned me. I remind Satan of the many, many miracles and divine provisions God has given me. Greater is He who is in me than he who is in the world. My life is a faith walk.

Part Two: Miracles Happen

My world is a faith walk.
I've learned to hear God's voice and to listen closely.
My world is supernatural, living miracle after miracle.

Miracle on 98th Street

Ask the animals. They will teach you.
Job 12:7-10

Our world is overflowing with miracles. They are everywhere for those who have eyes to see them. I've seen so many people touched by the healing hand of God. I will never, ever forget the first physical healing I witnessed. It was deeply personal and completely surprised me. Rosie was my very elderly, sweet English bulldog. She'd been with me through thick and thin. Rosie dried my every tear through the loss of Mom, homelessness, and so much more. She was a little clown and brought joy to my world.

Rosie had been almost blind for eight years with only slight peripheral vision. That little bit of vision helped her, along with a keen sense of smell. She lost her hearing three years after her vision went. I thought she was being stubborn. Bulldogs can be that way. Her vet said she was deaf, quite possibly stubborn, but definitely deaf. Rosie had been battling repeated bladder infections for two years and was well into her teens. She'd far outlived the typical life span of an English bulldog. I had spoiled and pampered Rosie her entire life and in turn, she had spoiled Julian and me.

Most nights, Rosie woke me up to go outside. This night was different. When she squatted, pure blood came out and Rosie collapsed on the front lawn and began shaking. She was having a seizure. It was the middle of the night. I was so afraid and couldn't bear the thought of losing her. I sat on the grass with her in my lap as I tried to calm her. Her shaking stopped, and she stood up but immediately fell again. Her back legs appeared paralyzed and buckled under her. I wondered if she had suffered a stroke. I'm not sure how I lifted that sixty-pound tank, but I did and brought her into the house.

That night, I lay with Rosie. As I tried to comfort her, I cried out to God. I thanked Him for caring about my every need for so long, including my sweet baby girl. I thanked Him for the wonderful life she'd had and the joy and comfort she'd brought Julian and me. I remembered all of her tutus and painted nails and the fun we'd had. I remembered her chasing after Julian as he skated on the half pipe. I remembered her chasing after Julian and his friends when they were shooting hoops and how she'd crush basketballs in a split second! I begged God to please take her painlessly as she slept in my arms. I couldn't bear the thought of having her put to sleep. I prayed for His mercy.

When I woke up the next morning, I heard Rosie lapping up water from her bowl in the kitchen. She was not paralyzed and very alive. In my excitement, I shouted her name. She came running. Did she just hear me? I loved on her, and she bounced around, kissing me as she did. She seemed to hear me. I went into my bedroom and closed the door and called her name. She came running!

Room after room, she responded to my voice. Rosie had supernaturally regained the hearing she'd lost five years before. I asked her if she was ready to go outside, and she ran to the door! When I opened it, she stopped with two paws inside and two paws outside suspended on the small step. She stayed that way for a moment, and then began barking. She hopped onto the brick entry and barked up a storm at the potted flowers outside. My blind dog had just seen flowers for the first time in eight years! Instinctively, I said, "It's okay, Rosie" as she barked, and she looked right up to me again!

She sashayed in her wiggle-butt style to the front yard and squatted with no sign of blood. Suddenly, she noticed her reflection in the hubcap of my car. She ran to it and barked at herself! We went inside, and I FaceTimed Julian in Seattle. He talked to her through the iPad and couldn't believe what he saw. We laughed, and I was in tears. Abba had healed my dog. Rosie and I visited Dr. Lopez, her vet. The recap of the night astonished him. Sometimes things just can't be explained, he said. I told him that I believed God had healed her. He smiled warmly at me, and I noticed the cross he wore around his neck.

Rosie and I had another wonderful year together. Then the day came when she asked to go. It was a peaceful decision. I lay beside Rosie as

Dr. Lopez gave her a relaxant. He is one of the kindest men I've ever known. He said she would be unable to blink or move and assured me she had no anxiety or pain. He left us alone. I asked God if dogs went to heaven and to make sure she knew how much I loved her.

Rosie lay motionless for about fifteen minutes, not even blinking. Dr. Lopez returned and asked if I was ready. Through tears, I nodded yes. Suddenly, Rosie lifted her head, her ears perked, and she looked up to the ceiling. She cocked her head from the right to the left, back and forth like a little curious owl as she gazed on. Everyone was startled when she moved. She had not even blinked in over fifteen minutes. Then she turned to me, licked me on the face, and laid her head down and took her last breath – without the planned euthanasia. We all cried. God showed me He was there with me and taking Rosie home with Him. She had done her job here on earth.

Harvey

But he was wounded for our transgressions,

he was bruised for our iniquities;

the chastisement of our peace was upon him;

and with his stripes we are healed.

Isaiah 53:5

My landlord, Harvey, was an extraordinarily wealthy Jewish man who was accustomed to being in control of his world. Occasionally, he'd whirl up in his Excalibur to check on his properties. Harvey didn't like to replace old dilapidated things but preferred a handyman to bandage them until they completely fell apart. My water heater was one of them. It kept going out and leaving me with a cold shower time and again.

When the water heater went out for the third time, I was at my wit's end. The lack of hot water frustrated me, and I allowed my emotions to take over. I'm a calm, patient person, but this time I told Harvey I was upset. He was completely quiet. Suddenly, I realized Harvey was crying! I felt horrible and asked if he was okay. Harvey sobbed as he told me his six-year-old granddaughter had awakened in terrible pain and was urinating blood. They had rushed her to the hospital where tests had shown the unthinkable. That little girl had a massive tumor and had gone into kidney failure as she slept. She had been airlifted to a pediatric hospital where they had confirmed everything. She was being prepped for surgery as we spoke. The family was in shock and was prepared for the worst. Harvey broke down and said, "She's only six years old. Why can't it be me with cancer?"

God asked me to pray for her at that moment. I'd never prayed for healing in front of anyone before and was apprehensive and felt shy. Harvey was a nonmessianic Jew who didn't like me so much. I was nervous but asked him if I could pray. He stammered saying yes. God's words flowed from my mouth. I asked Him to heal Harvey's granddaughter in Jesus' name. Harvey sobbed and thanked me.

A few hours later, a repairman showed up with a new water heater. Harvey called me the next morning and asked if I enjoyed the hot shower. I felt like a jerk. I thanked him and asked about his granddaughter. He burst into tears again and shouted, "It is a miracle! They went in to remove the tumor and to try to save one kidney, and, Ada, it was gone! There was no tumor! There is no bleeding! She is coming home now, and she is fine! It is a miracle!" Truly I tell you I was speechless . . . completely speechless. Harvey said, "Your prayer was magic." I said, "No, Harvey, it's Jesus and He heals!" Harvey has called me just to chat several times. Harvey's curiosity about the living God who heals is leading him straight into the arms of Jesus.

Mary Jane

With man this is impossible,
but with God all things are possible. – Jesus
Matthew 19:26

One day, I was finishing with a regular client and looked up to see Mary Jane walking up the path to my door. She looked full of anguish and pain as she came in, head down, and quietly took a seat. She was frail and didn't look spiritually healthy. I knew she wasn't there for just hair. We discussed design, and I started working on her hair color. I asked her about her life.

Mary Jane's daughter had just given birth to her third child. Mary Jane was flying up to care for the first two grandchildren. She explained that her daughter's pregnancy had been extremely difficult and that she had almost lost the baby multiple times. Her daughter's body had been "rejecting" the baby from early pregnancy. She had suffered multiple "failed miscarriages," and then she began to get very sick. She had been diagnosed with gestational lupus. Mary Jane said her daughter's vital organs began to shut down when she was rushed to a hospital and then put into a medically induced coma. She went into labor almost two months early while in a coma. Somehow, she survived delivering the baby naturally, and a team of neonatologists were there to take over with the baby. Her precious baby boy was born with perforated lungs. He could not hold or process any air on his own. Her son-in-law asked to have his baby boy put on life support until she was able to meet and say goodbye to their baby boy. Mary Jane's daughter was dangling by a thread to life. Her prognosis was not good and her vital organs were continuing to slow down.

Mary Jane was going to care for her two grandchildren while her son-in-law stayed with her daughter and baby boy, both on life support. She told me all of this with a straight and sober face. I had stopped my work with her hair and could not hold back my tears. She looked at me and broke down crying too. Through her tears, Mary Jane said she had not done anything with her hair or for herself since her daughter's condition had become so serious. She expressed how hard it was to be so many miles away from her daughter and to feel so hopeless and scared. As she began explaining that she was trying to look normal for the other kids, I realized she was worried that I'd think less of her for having her hair done. I told her God brought her for prayer that day and that I felt she was exactly where she needed to be. Her concern of judgment broke my heart, and instantly, I left the back of the chair and kneeled in front of her. I took her hands, looked up to her, and asked her if she believed in God. When she said yes, I asked her if I could pray.

Mary Jane looked into my eyes, and tears flowed for both of us as God gave me His words to pray. I asked Him to intervene and to save her daughter and her grandson's life. As Mary Jane was leaving, I invited her to a book study I had every week and told her she wasn't ever alone. My heart broke for her. I didn't want our time to end.

That was Wednesday. Friday, she would be leaving to see her daughter. Six days later, on the following Tuesday, during my book study, there was a knock at my door. Assuming it was one of us, I yelled, "Come on in" as we gathered around the table. It was Mary Jane. She was glowing. She quickly announced that a miracle had occurred.

Mary Jane hadn't gone to her daughter's home. Her daughter's vitals had suddenly normalized, and she had awakened from her coma. It was impossible. Her body, vital signs, and organs were functioning normally. Additionally, her baby boy was taken out of sedation and removed from life support. Her daughter wanted to meet him and hold him in her arms as he went to heaven. Mary Jane wept as she told us he is breathing normally, without any medical assistance. His lungs are healed. Then she said they were both home! I burst into tears. Everyone at the table knew this was a testimony to another miracle, but they didn't know the details. Mary Jane sat down. We didn't have a book study that day. We listened to a joyous grandmother's account of God's amazing healing.

God speaks everywhere that there are ears to hear

One morning, I awakened with a strong desire to attend water fitness classes. A huge waterpark near my home had exactly what I was looking for. I jumped right into the class and met women of all ages and fitness levels. Immediately, I felt right at home. I was only in the pool a few times when God began to stir things up.

In the pool, I met a woman named Mary. Her spot was right by mine. One morning, Mary and her friends were discussing Jewish holidays. God nudged me to share a few miracle testimonies, and they listened closely. Mary was agitated one morning and wasn't herself. She was discussing problems with the sale of one of her homes with her friends. God told me to pray for her, yet I was thinking, *She's Jewish and may not want my prayers, and there's so many people, and I feel weird and, and, and . . .*

Having God push me to pray publicly was new to me. Meanwhile, God ignored the excuses I was making to get out of praying. As we got out of the pool, I approached Mary and told her that God had told me to pray for her. Mary agreed with a surprised and reluctant look. I took her hands and prayed as I asked for His favor. She was looking closely at me and I finished, asking in Jesus' name. She shook my hands loose and left quickly. Mary and her friends said very little to me after that day.

One day, Mary asked if I remembered praying for her and said, "You brought me good luck!" Mary told me her doctors had found a tumor on her uterus. She was having surgery followed by immediate chemotherapy and radiation. She asked if I would pray for her the next day privately. I felt God's push, saying, *Pray now, not tomorrow, and do it in front of everyone.* I prayed God's words over Mary and gave her my contact information. She called me after her surgery. Her chemotherapy and radiation were canceled because the tumor was determined to be contained and benign. She celebrated in the moment but in time seemed to forget that Jesus had healed her. She came to me a few months later with a financial request for prayer and told me I was her good luck charm. I loved Mary but in my heart I was sad that she did not recognize Jesus after the amazing miracles she'd received.

Jesus reminded me how long it had taken to get my attention! I told Mary that I wasn't her good luck charm, but that it was Jesus. I said, "He's after your heart." She returned to the pool the next week, and He had blessed her again by answering that prayer right away. Several months went by when Mary came to me distraught. She had been diagnosed with breast cancer. She asked me to pray for her and invited me to her home for lunch. Mary asked Jesus into her heart that day after we ate. She prayed with me, and when you look at her you now you see His light. She's become my special friend, and Mary has blessed me profoundly. Today she is a healthy, cancer-free believer. Mary told me when she can't find words to pray, she says, "I trust you, Jesus." When she told me this, I cried.

Mary is one of so many in that pool. Breast cancer has been healed twice. A paralyzed stroke victim normalized overnight and is now playing golf. Back pain vanished. An attempted suicide in a young teenager was halted before it was too late, and a family is walking in their freedom. A seriously depressed, abused woman found God and strength. Debilitating migraines vanished in a second. A suicidal and depressed young man found hope in Jesus and a reason to go on. The miracles in that pool were amazing.

God is everywhere we have ears to hear and eyes to see. I walked the "lazy river" in that waterpark alone every morning. It became like a prayer closet to me, outside in nature. People love to walk there with a strong current at their back propelling them forward. They walk in groups, laughing, splashing, and having fun. Sometimes they let the current carry them and just float quickly around that river. I'm usually the only one who chooses to walk against the current. It's difficult to do and takes focus. Without focus, it would knock me backward.

Every day, people invite me to join them and walk with the current. I believe they think I'm nuts. But the benefits are just too awesome! Besides the obvious workout, it's a great prayer time outside, alone with God. Beautiful ripples in the water create a reflective painting in motion at the bottom of the pool. The top glistens and sparkles like diamonds. It's gorgeous and in fluid movement. I leave physically and spiritually refreshed and ready for my day. One day, I turned around and walked with the current for a few moments to chat with a friend. The designs disappeared! There were no ripples or diamonds in sight and no sparkle. When I turned around, it was all back. I did this multiple times in multiple areas around that river. I just couldn't believe my eyes. God spoke to me in those moments. God told me that following Him is hard. People will laugh and make fun of you. People will gossip and speak slander against you for doing so. Following Jesus takes focus, perseverance, and dedication. But, just like the water, by doing so there is beauty dancing everywhere! God will never, ever leave you or forsake you. He will guide you through that narrow gate to Him. Sadly, many miss the beauty of the struggle and the amazing miracles along the way—the eternal embrace of His real love.

Matthew 7: 13-14:Enter by the narrow gate; for wide is the gate and broad is the way that leads to destruction, and there are many who go by it. Because a narrow gate is narrow and difficult is the way which leads to life, and there are few who find it.

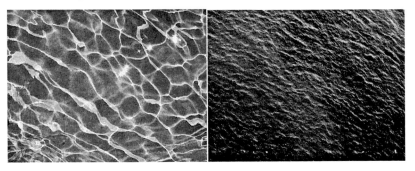

225

I also attend aerobics with Mary and many others in a huge pool with an island in the center. When the park opens after class every day, hundreds of kids are in that pool, jumping off the island. Ricardo teaches the class from the island. One day, I was marveling at how incredibly peaceful it was. The peace was palpable when someone shouted "Look up!" Two rainbows arched above us. Birds sang and butterflies fluttered over our heads. It was just so cool. I refocused on Ricardo, who continued to lead the class from the island. Suddenly, I noticed a very tall single-stem, delicate rose-type flower growing right from the center of that island. It had not been there the day before or it would surely have been picked or trampled by the hundreds of kids who came there daily. It was eighteen to twenty inches tall. God was trying to get my attention again.

I felt God say, "Sudden. Sudden miracles. Sudden joy." After class ended, I took these pictures, but the rainbows had faded. I learned this flower is called a Hurricane Rose and is known for its SUDDEN flowers that have a delicate stem usually stretching eighteen to twenty-six inches tall overnight! God led me to read Isaiah 35, and I was profoundly blessed. I encourage you to do the same.

Camille

I've always dreamed of visiting New York City. For years, I'd wanted to go to Times Square Church and experience the city's art and culture. One day, God surprised me by providing plane tickets and a hotel in NYC. My trip was amazing. I experienced many divine and incredible moments with wonderful people. But there is one moment that I could never have been prepared for. I will never, ever forget Camille.

I was with a dear friend, and every day we would set out with plans and our walking shoes on. I never carried cash, but that day I knew I was going to need it. We boarded the subway with a mapped-out day ahead of us. Somehow, we were so deep in conversation that we missed our stop and went way past our original destination. We decided to just go with it and changed our plans. We visited the World Trade Center and then wandered into the Financial District. It happened again. We walked quite a ways along a street, laughing and chatting, when we realized we were walking in the wrong direction.

I saw many homeless men, women, and children. After being homeless myself, my discernment is keen. As we walked along, suddenly we came upon a woman who sat huddled on the ground, leaning against a wall, and cradling her precious son. She was cold, hungry, and very broken. She whimpered, "Please help me" through her tears to businessmen with briefcases as they whisked by, too busy to look at her. As my friend and I walked at a fast pace, my eyes caught those of the woman on the ground as we passed her by. Instantly, I stopped and took my cash out, praying as I did.

I turned around and walked back to the woman. Our eyes met, and I handed her the money. Then I sat with her and held her and prayed as she cried in my arms. I told her I understood, that I'd been homeless for twenty-two months. I shared how God had provided for my every need and that He was going to do the same for her. I told her Jesus loved her and then I dissolved into tears as she spoke. Camille told me that she loved Jesus too but she felt He'd forgotten her. Through tears, I explained how Jesus told me to bring money with me that day and then took me way out of my way to bring me directly to her. I told her that Jesus took me straight to her because He loves her and her son so very much. Camille promised to call me, and I pray that she does. I will never, ever forget Camille. She and her son profoundly blessed me.

You see, Camille was not crazy or a druggie or dirty or all the other stigmas we place around the homeless. Camille was someone's daughter, sister, and best friend. I pray I always have His eyes, hands, and feet to serve as He has served me so incredibly. It's time we all slow down and care for each other. Nothing else matters in the end. Camille so profoundly blessed me. All my life, I'd dreamed of going to New York City. God showed me why that day: Her name was Camille.

Part Three: Finding Answers

Understanding Spirituality

My journey has had many twists and turns that I could have never in my wildest dreams imagined. I've had many suddenlies. Sudden Loss. Sudden Terror. Sudden Grief. Sudden Miracles. Sudden Breakthroughs and Sudden Joy. I've learned that it was in my darkest moments that God's light shined in undeniable brightness. I love Jesus and will never turn back. I've been blessed with miracles too abundant to count. But I must tell you that with this heightened spiritual awareness comes the reality of darkness.

In this world, there is light and there is darkness. There is good and there is evil. God is real and so is Satan. God comes to bring life and abundance. He is truth. He is love. He came to set the captives free. Satan has only one mission: to kill, steal, and destroy anyone or anything that is a threat to his agenda. That means marriages, relationships, families, ministries, health, finances, and so much more. Satan seeks to have you oppressed, depressed, hopeless, joyless, sorrowful, worried, stressed out, and defeated. He would love to have you float aimlessly through life never knowing your purpose. He takes joy in hiding your destiny and the very reason that God created you. He's been trying to choke the life out of me since I was a very little girl.

I've grown stronger, and God has healed me from unthinkable pain. As I learn to walk in this freedom, the attacks against me have morphed into something new. Satan hates that I know who I am. I am a fearless warrior Jesus and His beloved daughter. I know that absolutely no weapon formed against me will prosper. I take the authority God has given me very seriously. My authority in Christ and yours came at a great cost: Jesus' death on a cross. Satan knows the end of the story; he is defeated. But he also knows most people are absolutely clueless about the very power that dwells within them. Satan goes after that weakness. Your ignorance can be fatal if you allow it.

Freedom comes from walking in a heightened awareness and reality, from knowing the truth. Blind people are people who choose to skip along in life with their heads in the sand. I've met many believers living in sadness and bondage. They think they shouldn't acknowledge the devil. Many believe the lie that Satan can't attack a Christian. Some are afraid of him, or they deny that Satan exists. These blind people are Satan's greatest assets, and he uses them to wage war against their very families unbeknownst to them. Satan's greatest lie is convincing people that he isn't real. This refusal to acknowledge his existence is seen in not only individuals, but entire churches. They refuse to believe he exists or holds any power to infiltrate their souls.

Do not be fooled. Satan hides in church pews everywhere. He sings on worship teams, and he can preach the word from the pulpit eloquently. He knows Scripture far better than you or I do. He's been practicing for thousands of years. Not only has he been practicing it, but he has a key role in many of the books in the Bible. He has lived the historical documentation we read in the Bible.

You can't outsmart Satan on your own. Only Christ in you defeats him. A spirit-filled believer knows the power we have in the double-edged sword, the word of God. His word will cut out what needs to go and heal what remains. But never forget, the devil tested and tormented Jesus Christ Himself in the wilderness with the twisted word of God. It is Christ in us who holds all the power. Never forget that greater is He who is in you than he who is in the world.

We must recognize that we are three parts: body, soul, and spirit. We are spiritual beings temporarily in a body with the king of kings living inside of us. Our body is the outermost man, the flesh and blood that we see, and our five senses. Our soul is our inner man. Our soul is our mind, our will, and our emotions. Our soul is our intellect, our feelings, and our personality. Our soul is what Satan loves to attack with legions of demons ready to tear us down. It's in our soul that inner pain is felt. For example, it is our soul that experiences oppression, depression, hopelessness, defeat, lust, evil thoughts, hate, division, bitterness, and unforgiveness, to name a few.

But our spirit or innermost man is what connects us to God in us, the Holy Spirit. Our spirit or innermost man is where we find intuition or discernment and revelation. It is where we receive insight from God, who is the Holy Spirit. Our spirit is where we commune with God. The Holy Spirit communes with our spirit and dwells within us. We are body, soul and spirit.

God heals. He resurrects broken bodies, broken minds, shattered hearts, and fractured lives. He does this *if* we allow Him to. It is a breaking process that is difficult and sometimes very painful to walk through. All pride has to go to allow the God to steer us. This is what a spirit-led believer is walking out. He brings great joy into the process of letting go and letting God.

Sitting in church on Sunday and listening to a feel-good message will not equip you for the days that lie ahead and the onslaught that Satan can throw at you, your family, and your loved ones. Our family in Christ, our covering and gathering together, is very important. This can be our support and offer us a shoulder to lean our heads on, but warfare is real and in the end, you must be able to defend yourself and fight for your family. You must arm yourself with the word of God. Your faith will soar to levels you never imagined as you immerse yourself in the word of God.

Often, I am asked how I hear God. People mistakenly think that hearing God's voice is a special gift that only a few have access to. This is not true! If you don't hear God's voice, it's because you don't read His Word. I was very intimidated the first time I picked up a Bible. It seemed overwhelming to me to be able to read and understand it. I started to read the book of Matthew first. Suddenly one day, it came alive to me. It is God who brings understanding and clarity to you. All you need to do is ask Him. He's there and waiting upon you to take ahold of His outstretched hand. He will guide you and teach you. As you read, God begins to speak to you in every circumstance in your life in a still, small voice and prompting in your spirit. God yearns for that intimacy with you. He loves you more than you will ever be able to comprehend.

You must equip yourself and those you love. We must embrace all spirituality to walk in wholeness and truth. God is love. God is all that is good. Satan is the lack and complete void of love and all that is good. You may find it hard to understand this next chapter, but it's the truth. The devil is real; he's also a defeated foe. I live and walk in a place of complete protection. That protection did not come from a court of law. That protection doesn't come from a partner by my side. My walk has been set apart and at times painfully alone. Do I dream of having a strong, Spirit-filled husband beside me as my protector? The answer is yes. But I know that Jesus Christ will always be my Forever Order of Protection.

Darkness is Real

Be alert and of sober mind.
Your enemy the devil prowls around like a roaring lion
looking for someone to devour. 1 Peter 5:8

The thief comes only to steal and kill and destroy;
I have come that they may have life, and have it to the full.
John 10:10

I didn't know anything about supernatural warfare. God always brings exactly what you need at the exact perfect time. Not only are Gods ways always higher, they are always right on time. One day, I was painting and worshipping when suddenly a link appeared on my iPad and my iPad's music stopped. I clicked the link. There before me was a man sharing his testimony of walking out of devil worshiping and into the arms of Jesus. I was riveted to the screen. As I watched as paint dried on my brush, ruining it. His testimony started connecting dots for me instantly. My childhood, my family problems, Damien, falling and breaking bones, the dog bite—everything started fitting together like a completed jigsaw puzzle.

This man is an evangelist and an expert on spiritual warfare. When the program ended, I immediately purchased his books and a CD set. I consumed them quickly and began learning. His books led to more books and a deeper understanding of the bible. God provides for our every single need. I reflected on my life and knew He had protected me over and over for many years. Now He was preparing me for such a time as this.

On October 31, 2015, I took my dog, Sadie, for a routine walk like we did multiple times a day. This day was different. It was midmorning and like most days, we were the only ones on the street. As we walked along the sidewalk, I noticed two men ahead of me. It was odd because I'd been looking down the street just moments ago and hadn't seen anyone. I had looked down at Sadie because she had run back to me nervously. Then I had looked back up and saw the men seeming to come from nowhere.

They were only about six feet in front of me. They were on opposite sides of the sidewalk and were facing each other with their bodies, but their heads were turned, both men staring at me. They looked like a father and son. The younger one stood with a skateboard flipped up against his leg, wheels still spinning. I noticed how odd it was that I didn't hear the familiar sound of a skateboard on cement. They both stared at me menacingly and didn't say a word to each other.

I felt the urge to turn back toward home, but I kept walking not breaking my stride and not wanting to show any fear *or* have my back to them. I prayed under my breath as I approached them. The glaring looks at me became very unsettling as Sadie and I drew near. Sadie was not her normal self and was panting loudly. As I quietly prayed I stared the older one straight into his eyes as I passed. His eyes were dark and void. I thought of Damien's eyes and said, "God bless you" as I passed by. I only took a few steps beyond them when I suddenly turned around to face them. They were gone. Two huge black snakes were fighting each other in the middle of the sidewalk where they'd stood. Keep in mind, from the moment I saw them the first time, to the moment I turned and saw two snakes, only a minute or so had passed.

For the first time, I was witnessing a physical manifestation of the spiritual darkness that had been trying to kill me. I quickly took inventory around me and noticed that the street was extremely quiet. No cars, busses, bikes, or walkers. Not a soul was in sight. As the two large black snakes fought on the sidewalk in front of me, I quickly ran to the other side of the street and continued praying. I was afraid and now praying loudly, walking very quickly back to my home.

Suddenly, another man came racing toward me on a bike. He wore black pants, long black sleeves, black gloves, and a black stocking cap. It was in the high seventies outside, not glove and hat weather. There's a bike path along the entire street, but he raced toward me on the sidewalk. I continued praying fervently. As he approached, I grabbed Sadie and jumped off the sidewalk or he would have ran us over. I thought he was wearing a mask but realized that it was deep burnlike scars that covered his entire face. They were purplish, shiny, and thick. Two holes sat on his face where there should have been a nose. His face dripped in sweat. I stared into dead black eyes as he passed by me not breaking his speed. His eyes didn't seem human.

I sprinted back to my condo carrying Sadie and praying loudly. I deadbolted the door behind me and dropped down, sitting with my back against the door, breathless with Sadie in my lap. My mind and spirit were racing. So was my heart. God brought to my mind the severe burns my dad had suffered before I was born—burns so deep that he'd needed skin grafts. God reminded me that the sweat glands are destroyed with burns as deep as these. The face with the black hat had poured sweat through extremely severe scarring.

God calmed me within minutes. He gave me His peace. He showed me that truly no weapon formed against me would prosper. This was a smokescreen. The devil was trying his best to scare me but had no power over me. The devil had tried to kill me many times but couldn't succeed. He tormented me with fear, but he lost that battle. He was pushing me again and now to new limits showing me sudden physical manifestations.

It happened again. On May 13, 2016, I awoke many times during the night to intense nightmares. I felt a physical heaviness in my bed. Although my head was only inches from the headboard, I had the sensation of a large man leaning on the pillow behind my head. At moments, I'd feel his hot breath on my neck. I can't remember any details of my dreams only that I just kept waking with extreme panicky fear, finding it hard to breathe. I felt like I was being chased and out of breath and strangled at the same time. I hadn't felt this kind of primal fear in a very long time. I stayed in bed and resisted the urge to jump up and turn on the lights. At moments, I felt like I was being held down and couldn't move. I wasn't sure if I was dreaming or awake. I prayed myself through this strange sensation.

When morning finally came, I was standing at my bathroom sink and I couldn't believe what I saw in the mirror: fingerprint bruises on my upper arms. The bruises remained for over a week. They were sore and deep and carried no explanation except the supernatural. Satan is real.

I was given the opportunity to attend a spiritual warfare conference lead by Pastors Alexander and Sandra Sarraga. They have a wonderful church in Orlando, Florida, called Champions City Church and a Global Evangelistic Outreach called Voice of Fire. On the opening night of this three day conference I met Pastors Alexander and Sandra. Somehow we made an extraordinary connection through the conference. I was profoundly blessed by the Holy Spirit that dominated their teaching. It culminated with a Sunday service given at Champions City Church. God spoke to me and told me that they would be the spiritual parents I needed and to glean all that I could from His faithful and wonderful sevants. He told me I would be working closely with both of them.   I saw Jesus all over them and was thrilled when they asked me to join them on a seven-day conference they were giving in Japan.

Sudden Detour

On February 28, 2017, a few weeks before my planned trip to Japan, I met a friend for lunch. We sat outside surrounded by lush vegetation and bright colorful flowers on a beautiful Florida afternoon. When we finished, we hugged each other goodbye, both of us feeling blessed by our time together. I hopped into my little car and she into hers to head for home. I started to put the top down but changed my mind because I had several stops to make before heading home.

I secured the top back up and pulled out onto a very busy main drag through the city. I was only a few blocks away, on the far right of three lanes heading north with a large island separating me from the three southbound lanes. I was moving with traffic at forty-five miles per hour. Suddenly, without any warning, a southbound car turned left in front of me. I didn't have time to brake. I saw a flash of brown traveling in front of me a fraction of a second before impact. I slammed into the side of the car. My airbag exploded, and I saw us flipping through the air. I didn't know if I was flipping or if it was the other car. Then everything went black.

I awoke to a man gently carrying me from my car to the side of the road. He laid me down in the grass. I was in so much pain I couldn't breathe. I opened my eyes and what I saw was like a stylized film playing out in front of me. The entire scene was blurred and foggy with the exception of this man's dark skin and a gold chain that wrapped around his neck. The chain was holding a dangling gold cross. The cross sparkled as it caught the sunlight. God spoke to me in that moment. He said, "Be still. Be at peace. I have sent him for you. I am with you." Then the man started to pray.

I heard a woman's voice praying behind me. Pain wracked my body, but a peace that surpasses all understanding enveloped me. As I lay on a stretcher, I could feel every single bump as paramedics jolted it into the ambulance. With every move, I felt like I was being stabbed. The pain was intense, yet I felt superpeaceful and safe. In the emergency room, staff gave me morphine for pain and began to run many tests. People scrambled around me as I lay on the stretcher in the hallway staring at the ceiling. They admitted me after many tests. As I lay there trying to comprehend what had just happened, I remembered that a man had put a piece of paper with his name and phone number on it in my purse as they'd wheeled me into the ambulance. He had said to please call him if I needed anything.

My car was totaled. There is absolutely no way I should've survived that accident. I was told my car even caught fire. I was very battered and bruised. I suffered a severed sternum, my shoulder was torn in multiple places, I had severely bruised and fractured bones in my arms, my knee was torn and broken in multiple places, and discs were ruptured and bulging in my neck. I had sustained extremely painful and deep abdominal and chest contusions. Even my toe nails shattered and split from the impact. I awoke on the second day with black eyes from where my glasses had broken off of my face. My vision was blurred from a brain concussion and suspected retinal tear.

As I was being released from the hospital, the surgeon said my shoulder and knee would require surgery. I was told that for ten to twelve additional weeks, I would not be allowed to bend my knee at all or drive. My trip to Japan was to occur in four weeks. My heart sank and darkness attempted to blanket over me. I reminded myself that I knew that Jesus was with me. He'd brought me comfort and peace from a dangling gold chain and a soft, gentle but strong voice, praying for me on the side of a road. I decided to find that piece of paper and call the angel God had sent to me.

His name is Robert. Robert is a serious man of God with his own church in New York City. Robert also has planted hundreds of churches in India and China. Robert and I both were choked up when we spoke. He told me that his wife and two children had held hands and prayed around me when they saw me. He saw Jesus in me the same way as I saw Jesus in him. This is a wonderful and divine connection from my Father that is just beginning to unfold.

You see, in ALL things God will get the glory! There is no devil in hell that can stand between God and His chosen ones.

In a flash of a second, your life can take a turn or make a sudden change too. In one second, it could be too late or an angel could appear before you. I pray each and every person reading this comes to know Jesus as intimately as I do. His arms are open wide waiting for you to choose Him.

Every single one of us is created with a purpose. We are created with a divine destiny. Our heavenly Father knew us as He formed us in our mother's womb. He was with us in our past. He is with us in our present, and He is waiting for us in our future. He is the Alpha and the Omega, the beginning and the end. He is not a vengeful God who lives in punishment. He doesn't condemn with guilt and heaviness. His Holy Spirit comes in and convicts our heart and then gently heals us from the inside out. He's not a religion you visit for an hour on Sunday. He is real. He wants a relationship with you. He wants your heart.

God has given me a second chance, and He will do the same for you. He rescued me from the mouth of the lion more than once. He prepared me for such a time as this. You are reading this by divine appointment. It is not happenstance. It is not serendipity. It is divine. Life is full of suddenlies. Life seems sudden to us. Rape, murder, cancer, suicide, oppression, depression, death, divorce, and even bankruptcy can suddenly change everything. So can finding God's purpose for your life, God's unique destiny He created just for you.

It's sudden. When you meet Jesus Christ, everything changes suddenly. I had to be a seriously broken woman to meet Him personally. I pray that you look up before you hit bottom. For when you do, you will find Him suddenly in front of you waiting for you to take His hand.

John 10:10: The thief does not come except to steal, and to kill, and to destroy. I have come that they may have life, and that they may have it more abundantly.

Isaiah 54:17: No weapon formed against you shall prosper,

And every tongue which rises against you in judgment You shall condemn. This is the heritage of the servants of the Lord.

Resources

* 911 Do not be afraid to use it.

* The National Domestic Violence Hotline 24/7 Confidential Support www.hotline.org

Safety Alert:

Computer use can be monitored and is impossible to completely clear. If you are concerned or afraid that your Internet usage might be monitored, call the National Domestic Violence Hotline at

1-800-799-7233

or TTY for the deaf, hard of hearing, or hearing impaired

1-800-787-3224

Ada Madison resides and works from her Orlando, Florida home. Madison speaks to groups of men and women openly and transpanently sharing her story. Her story has touched countless lives bringing healing, hope and faith-fueled inspiration. It is Ada's passion to not only help people to find their purpose and destiny, but to warn and help other women who are still struggling with the scars and pain of an abusive and deceptive relationship.

Follow Ada Madison's faith-fueled and colorful blog, FaithWalk, and see all of her art at:

www.AdaMadison.com

Contact Ada Madison at: ada@adamadison.com